EXPERIENCING BESSIE SMITH

The Listener's Companion
Gregg Akkerman, Series Editor

Titles in **The Listener's Companion** provide readers with a deeper understanding of key musical genres and the work of major artists and composers. Aimed at nonspecialists, each volume explains in clear and accessible language how to *listen* to works from particular artists, composers, and genres. Looking at both the context in which the music first appeared and has since been heard, authors explore with readers the environments in which key musical works were written and performed.

EXPERIENCING BESSIE SMITH

A Listener's Companion

John Clark

ROWMAN & LITTLEFIELD
Lanham • Boulder • New York • London

Published by Rowman & Littlefield
A wholly owned subsidiary of The Rowman & Littlefield Publishing Group,
Inc.
4501 Forbes Boulevard, Suite 200, Lanham, Maryland 20706
www.rowman.com

Unit A, Whitacre Mews, 26-34 Stannary Street, London SE11 4AB

British Library Cataloguing in Publication Information Available

Library of Congress Cataloging-in-Publication Data

Names: Clark, John, 1968- author.
Title: Experiencing Bessie Smith : a listener's companion / John Clark.
Description: Lanham : Rowman & Littlefield, 2017. | Series: Listener's companion | Includes
    bibliographical references and index.
Identifiers: LCCN 2017008576 (print) | LCCN 2017009065 (ebook) | ISBN 9781442243408
    (cloth : alk. paper) | ISBN 9781442243415 (electronic)
Subjects: LCSH: Smith, Bessie, 1894-1937—Criticism and interpretation.
Classification: LCC ML420.S667 C53 2017 (print) | LCC ML420.S667 (ebook) | DDC
    782.421643092—dc23 LC record available at https://lccn.loc.gov/2017008576

∞ ™ The paper used in this publication meets the minimum requirements of
American National Standard for Information Sciences Permanence of Paper
for Printed Library Materials, ANSI/NISO Z39.48-1992.

Printed in the United States of America

For my parents—John and Rita Clark—
who encouraged me to persevere in all things

CONTENTS

SERIES EDITOR'S FOREWORD

The goal of the Listener's Companion series is to give readers a deeper understanding of pivotal musical genres and the creative work of its iconic composers and performers. This is accomplished in an inclusive manner that does not necessitate extensive music training or elitist shoulder rubbing. Authors of the series place the reader in specific listening experiences in which the music is examined in its historical context with regard to both compositional and societal parameters. By positioning the reader in the real or supposed environment of the music's creation, the author provides for a deeper enjoyment and appreciation of the art form. Series authors, often drawing on their own expertise as both performers and scholars, deliver to readers a broad understanding of major musical genres and the achievements of artists within those genres as lived listening experiences.

It is with great pride and anticipation that the Listener's Companion series can now add blues to the list of topics covered. There were many possible angels that could have been approached for the genre but starting near the beginning with the great Bessie Smith was too scintillating to resist. As early as 1923, still in the early era of recorded music, Bessie enjoyed her first hits that nearly a century later reach across time with a stunning freshness and biting relevance. Whether it's the scorned-lover wailing of "Downhearted Blues," the double entendre cheekiness of "Need a Little Sugar in My Bowl," or the genre-crossing poignancy of her duets with jazz great Louis Armstrong, Bessie fully embodies the joy, sorrow, and "just livin' my life" attitude of the blues idiom.

Bessie's admirers include classic jazz vocalists Ella Fitzgerald and Billie Holiday, rockers Janis Joplin and the Band, rhythm and blues artists such as Queen Latifah, and thousands of fans across the world. In that spirit of both historical and contemporary relevance, the Listener's Companion welcomes author Dr. John Clark Jr. to share the story of Smith's music and times. I encourage you not only to enjoy Clark's highly engaging and non-jargon-filled narrative, but to seek out the original recordings (widely available on the Internet) and hear the beauty of her voice and conviction of her experience.

Gregg Akkerman

ACKNOWLEDGMENTS

I would like to thank many people for their help in writing this book. First, Judith Tick of Northeastern University initially inspired me to begin research on Bessie Smith when I was a graduate student at Brandeis University in the mid-1990s. Her thoughts and opinions (and writings) have been of great importance to me. My undergraduate adviser, Thomas Stoner, was also crucial in forming my thoughts about music history and how to approach jazz in particular. Guthrie Ramsey and Jeffrey Magee are both scholars who have been generous enough to give considered opinions on projects with which I have been involved during the last twenty years, and I have greatly appreciated their input.

Without the Internet, a project like this one would have taken decades—the ability to look things up, cross reference, and often simply listen to a rare recording at a moment's notice is a gift no scholar can fail to appreciate. Even with these vast resources available at the touch of a button, the help of dedicated librarians is still a vital component to research. Carolyn Johnson and June Ingram of Connecticut College Music Library have my eternal thanks for their diligence and patience in helping me unearth microfilm, copies of articles, rare books and recordings, as well as in providing support with databases, sympathy, and occasionally cookies.

Finally, all the musicians I work with on almost a daily basis have given me support and encouragement beyond measure, as well as a creative outlet and a practical application for my interest in jazz and blues history.

INTRODUCTION

Artistic originality is a difficult concept to define. What seems original to someone viewing a life's work from a distance of almost a century might not have seemed so to the artist's contemporaries and vice versa. Even the artist herself might not have viewed her work as being strikingly original or trailblazing, having been done in the service of commerce. Indeed, it was the rare performer of popular music during the first half of the twentieth century who viewed their work in terms of art rather than craft.

Until the beginning of the commercial recording era, performers were known to audiences outside their touring circle only through hearsay and accounts by contemporaries and critics. This doubtless enhanced the reputations of some while serving to bury many others in the mists of time. By the time film and sound recording were being marketed as entertainment to an eager public (both beginning roughly around 1900), most of the great names of music and drama of the nineteenth century were already gone, although a few such as Johannes Brahms and Sarah Bernhardt lived long enough to be immortalized, albeit at the end of their performing lives and not at the top of their game.

The rise of commercial reproduction on record for entertainment purposes coincided with the simultaneous development of the two most dominant musical tropes in twentieth-century popular music—blues and jazz. Although the beginnings of each form are irretrievably lost to history (both came from African American origins and in their initial phases were primarily oral traditions), the 1920s saw blues and jazz musicians create a body of recorded work that captured an early yet fully formed stage in their development. Although distinct forms with individual practitioners, repertoires, and performance traditions, blues and jazz were inseparable during this stage of development.

Of the two, it was blues that was regarded as a popular sensation first. By the early 1910s, sheet music was being produced using the word "blues" in the title and codifying the twelve-bar lyric and harmonic structures still in use today. The music itself had been around since at least the beginning of the century and probably well before that as well, but it was the appearance of printed music that generated interest in the form and style to bring it out of its cultural domain and into the mainstream. In African American culture at the time, these blues were both traditional elements of society (along the lines of folk music) and theatrical fare that combined with splashy traveling circus and tent shows. These shows (particularly circuses) were also sometimes performed for white audiences, introducing them to vernacular black music at a time when crossover was not usually an option.

Bessie Smith cut her professional teeth during the decade when blues was beginning to establish its cultural prominence and she was exposed to the first theatrical manifestations of the style. As a chorus girl, comedienne, and singer during the years before and after World War I, Smith was called on to perform a range of popular material including blues, and she honed her own performance style, which was informed by many elements of her upbringing. By 1923 when she began recording, Smith was already a seasoned performer who was respected for her singing beyond any other of her range of talents. It was a happy chance of fate that she was given the opportunity to record at the height of her abilities. Her popular success increased with her ever-expanding discography, making this one of the few confluences of talent, popularity, and recording success at the time.

Smith's recording career was important for more than just promotional reasons. Her recording director for the entire length of her association with Columbia was Frank Walker. He functioned not only as the producer of the sessions, but also as a booking agent for her tours during that period, her business manager, friend, and sometimes parent to the mercurial singer. Accounts left by Ruby Walker and Maud Smith (both relatives as well as employees of Bessie Smith) and musician

Elmer Snowden (Albertson 2003, 108) mention Walker in a flattering light and his later interviews show that he took an enthusiastic interest in her career. Unlike other record producers of the 1920s (for example, the white Ralph Peer of Okeh and African American J. Mayo Williams of Paramount), Walker did not overtly seek to profit from his clients by taking credit for their songs or publishing them himself. His role in Smith's professional life during the most popular time of her career has not been fully examined, although it seems clear that his influence was one of the most stable elements of her life.

Of Smith's contemporaries, only Ma Rainey, Ethel Waters, Alberta Hunter, and Clara Smith are similarly represented on records, and only Hunter and Waters exceed her length of career. One of Smith's greatest influences was Ma Rainey, who recorded a great deal for the small Midwestern Paramount label beginning a few months after Bessie Smith began recording for Columbia. Unfortunately, those sides are badly recorded and Rainey was at that point acknowledged as past her prime, although she remained a popular draw in person until she retired in the early 1930s. Clara Smith essentially shadowed Bessie Smith for most of her career at Columbia, using many of the same musicians, singing similar tunes, and even recording at the same time (including duets with her on three sides). Nevertheless, she was a shadow in other ways—virtually nothing is known of her life during the 1920s outside of her tours as reported in the African American press. Even the years leading up to her death in 1935 are sparsely documented.

Hunter transitioned from a blues and cabaret singer to an actress in the late 1920s, making a career in Europe for a time before retiring from show business in 1957 to become a nurse. With only a few public appearances before her retirement from nursing in 1977, she began a third career as a singer, reviving many of her old tunes as well as performing other jazz and popular material. Waters was the most consistently successful of these four contemporaries—after an immensely productive recording career, she found success both on Broadway and film in the 1930s and 1940s before branching out first to radio and then television in the 1950s. Her last decade (she died in 1977) was spent singing with the Billy Graham crusade and guesting on TV talk shows.

During the 1920s these four women made an aggregate total of more than five hundred recordings, which are, with very few exceptions, almost entirely forgotten today. Bessie Smith, on the other hand, made about 170 sides (including alternate takes and a film), all of which have been reissued numerous times since her death. Why has she been remembered and celebrated to such a degree when contemporaries with far longer careers and more full discographies are marginalized?

The answer to that question ultimately lies in the grooves of the records themselves and the story of Bessie Smith's personal and professional life, both of which were inextricably bound to them from 1923 until the end of her life.

TIMELINE

April 15, 1894 (possibly 1892)	Born in Chattanooga, Tennessee
1912	First professional appearance with Moses Stokes company
1912–1913	Duo act with Wayne "Buzzin'" Burton
1913–1914	Apprenticeship at the 81 Theater in Atlanta
1917–1918?	Marriage to Earl Love
1919	Headlines *Liberty Belle*
1920–1921	Moves to Philadelphia
January 1923	Participates in *How Come?*
February 1923	First recordings
April 1923	First contract with Columbia; recordings with Fletcher Henderson and his musicians; business arrangement with Frank Walker
June 7, 1923	Marriage to Jack Gee
summer 1923–winter 1924	Tour through Middle Atlantic States; first radio broadcast
March 1924	Second contract with Columbia
May–June 1924	Performances in Chicago (recounted by Ruby Walker)

January 1925	First recordings with Louis Armstrong
May 1925	First electric recordings; first recordings with a large band
fall 1925	*Harlem Frolics* tour; introduction of new railroad car
spring 1926	"Adoption" of Jack Gee Jr. and relocation of her family to Philadelphia
summer 1927	*Harlem Frolics* tour
April 1928	*Mississippi Days* show in New York; Van Vechten party
fall 1928	*Steamboat Days* show
May 1929	Participates in *Pansy* on Broadway
June 1929	Films *St. Louis Blues*
fall 1929	*Midnite Steppers* show and discovery of Jack Gee's affair with Gertrude Saunders and his involvement with her career (Chris Albertson dates this a year earlier)
1930	Jack Gee Jr. taken into state custody for two years
August 1930	*Happy Times*—one of her last big productions
ca. 1930	Beginning of relationship with Richard Morgan
November 1931	End of association with Columbia
November 1933	Final recording session
1934–1937	Appearances in clubs and theaters in New York City
September 26, 1937	Death while touring with *Broadway Rastus* in Clarksdale, Mississippi
1951	First LP release of Bessie Smith recordings (George Avakian)
1970	Tombstone provided for her grave by Juanita Hall and Janis Joplin

1971	First complete release of Bessie Smith recordings (John Hammond)
1972	Publication of Chris Albertson's *Bessie*
1992	First CD release of complete Bessie Smith recordings (Chris Albertson)
2003	Republication of Albertson's *Bessie*
2015	HBO film about the life of Bessie Smith: *Bessie*, starring Queen Latifah

I

CRAZY BLUES

On a hot summer evening just before the beginning of World War I someplace in the deepest part of the Gulf region a huge tent has magically appeared overnight. Handbills and posters have been put up all over town to advertise the appearance of a traveling show to the African American community that has been laboring in the fields for months to create a sustainable life for themselves. This is their time to kick back and be entertained, and a more particular audience could not be found.

During this time of segregation (some of the people in the audience were born before emancipation and most others were children or grandchildren of former slaves), black entertainment was an amazingly rich and complex mix of vernacular elements—gospel, minstrel, ragtime, marches, show tunes, folk music, and the relatively new but immensely popular blues were all present. These tent show troupes found that the recipe for success is variety. Each show included comedians, dancers, instrumental music, and singers, with the singers usually being the most popular draw. Every successful show had a vocalist who specialized in singing blues—the laments and celebrations carrying a deep personal meaning for each member of the sweating crowd in front of them.

However, this was not all they sang—each of the performers in these companies was a battle-tested professional able to answer the demands of this rural audience, as well as—during a different time of year—the more sophisticated entertainment desires of urban crowds in the chain of theaters presenting black vaudeville. What is missing from this picture is an actual record of what these entertainers did. African American performers of vernacular music and theater were, with very few exceptions, not given the opportunity to make records of films of the material that represented their livelihood. It was not until the 1920s that the conglomerates controlling sound and image recordings were finally convinced of the marketability of black show business.

THE ROOTS

The roots of the blues style and form reach back into the latter part of the nineteenth century, although documentation is sparse beyond some casual reminiscences of early performers. Though performance practice that we might today recognize as "bluesy" (using altered notes of the standard scale, textual themes of love and loss, standard chord progressions, interaction between vocal and instrumental performers) probably existed for many years before the turn of the century, it was not until about 1912 that blues was regarded as a standard form and stylistic approach. In terms of the standard twelve-bar form, the ragtime songs "One o' Them Things" (Leroy Smith and James Chapman, 1904) and "I Got the Blues" (Anthony Maggio, 1908) both contain strains built on the blues progression, and the Tin Pan Alley song "Oh You Beautiful Doll" (Seymour Brown and Nat D. Ayer, 1911) includes a verse in twelve-bar blues form.

In 1912 at least three songs were published either partly or entirely in twelve-bar blues form—"Dallas Blues" by Hart Wand, "Baby Seals Blues" by Artie Matthews, and "Memphis Blues" by W. C. Handy. It was this last number that eventually became popular enough to earn for its composer the title "father of the blues." Many early examples of published blues include sections not in the twelve-bar form; for example, both "Memphis Blues" and Handy's even more popular "St. Louis Blues" (1914) include sixteen-bar strains in addition to multiple blues choruses, suggesting the form of ragtime compositions from a slightly earlier period.

Following the unprecedented success of "The Memphis Blues" (helped by a popular recording by the Victor Band and James Reese Europe's performance of the song introducing the new "fox-trot" dance by the popular team of Vernon and Irene Castle), the form was codified into the familiar pattern of three lines of four measures each. Though these early examples of blues were largely through-composed and narrative, the style soon evolved into a text roughly in AAB form. For example, "St. Louis Blues" begins:

A. I hate to see the evening sun go down
A. Hate to see the evening sun go down
B. 'cause my baby, he done left this town (Handy 1949)

These three lines are supported by different chords that make use of some of the characteristic "blue notes"—usually the third, fifth, and seventh notes of the major scale in Western music are bent, or lowered in pitch, imparting the flavor recognized as "bluesy." The first line is primarily in the home key—in musical terms, the "I" chord around which the tonality is based, while the second line begins on the IV chord (based on the fourth note of the scale), returning to the I halfway through. The third line begins on the V chord, returning to I by the end of the line. Graphically, it would be represented this way if the piece is in the key of G (as is "St. Louis Blues"):

Notice that the text is only on the first half of each line—the second half (supported by the last two chords of each) was generally left "open" for instrumental responses and occasionally some vocal commentary or elaboration. This type of interaction (which was usually improvised) is an example of "call and response," a key component of much of African and African American music.

This is the basic structure and chord progression of the standard twelve-bar blues from Handy's time through the present, such landmarks of American popular music as "In the Mood" (popularized by Glenn Miller), "Hound Dog" (Big Mama Thornton and Elvis Presley), and "Rock and Roll" (Led Zeppelin) are based in part or whole on this

G	G	G	G
I hate to see the evening sun go down			
C	C	G	G
Hate to see the evening sun go down			
D	C	G	G
'cause my baby, he done left this town			

twelve-bar progression. Was this how blues singers and instrumentalists approached the music before Handy and his contemporaries began publishing their blues songs? Maybe or maybe not, but recordings of black musicians performing this material in this style were not made in any numbers until the 1920s, so performance practice during the blues developmental stage is speculative at best. Some pre-1920s recordings by black bands did feature blues songs but in either a formal setting (for example, the recordings by Handy's own band), a vaudeville/novelty approach (Wilbur Sweatman's groups), or outside the United States (the string band recordings made in England by Ciro's Club Coon Orchestra and the Versatile Four). All of these recordings were made after the publication of the first blues songs.

CLASSIC BLUES

A commonly held assumption is that during the first two decades of the twentieth century (before any vocal blues recordings were made), authentic blues was the exclusive domain of the illiterate, itinerant black male minstrel who sang of his own personal experience. This view has proven quite durable over the years and remains intact to some extent today, owing to the relative dearth of research on the early female singers prior to what came to be known as the Classic Blues era of the 1920s. In fact, women such as Bessie Smith and Ma Rainey were touring the tent show and circus circuits from the earliest years of the century and incorporating in their shows the blues-based material with which they came to be identified. It was these women who carried their interpretation of Country Blues to a national audience, creating the market that later led to blues-based jazz, rhythm and blues, and eventually rock and roll.

In 1920, a singer who had found popularity in numerous all-black theatrical shows became the first African American to make a recording of a popular song. Mamie Smith (1883–1946) had been touring the country on the black vaudeville circuit since the early years of the century and was known for her abilities as a comedienne, dancer, and singer. Her voice was not what today we would consider "bluesy," instead being clear and well projected with careful enunciation and phrasing. A polished stage performer, Smith was a favorite of African

American entrepreneur and songwriter/promoter Perry Bradford who, like many others in his field, was continually trying to "place" his songs with established artists, both in person and on record.

After much lobbying, Bradford was told by the director of the OKeh recording company that he would be allowed to record two of his original songs, provided that he get the popular white singer Sophie Tucker to sing them. When it was discovered that Tucker was under contract to another company, Bradford proposed that Mamie Smith record the tunes—a daring suggestion in those segregated times (Bradford 1965, 117–19). Smith's recordings of "That Thing Called Love" and "You Can't Keep a Good Man Down" (OKeh 4113, recorded February 14, 1920) were done with a white studio band and were popular songs of the day (rather than blues) but were an immediate success with African American audiences who previously had not been considered an economic factor by the recording industry. This success opened the door for other black popular singers to begin making records.

By 1920, the initial patents for phonograph recording technology had expired, opening the field to smaller companies such as OKeh to break into the industry. The smaller budgets of such companies influenced the accompaniments on records—rather than recording large wind bands or theater orchestras, companies now favored smaller, more flexible groups to back popular singers (Kenney 1999, 79).

CRAZY BLUES

Following the success of her initial releases, Mamie Smith was engaged to make more recordings for OKeh. The next was of Bradford's tune "Harlem Blues," which was retitled "Crazy Blues." Supported by a small band (called her "Jazz Hounds") of black instrumentalists, including the important early jazz cornet stylist Johnny Dunn, Smith here became the first black singer to record a vocal blues in the United States. Though not really a blues singer in the traditional sense, Smith was a development of a tradition known as "coon shouter." This style was founded by white female singers who would sing in blackface, pronouncing lyrics of love and loss (often in black dialect) with a loudly declamatory delivery. The success of singers such as Tucker and May Irwin in this style opened the field for Mamie Smith and black vaudeville singers to find success and some measure of acceptance by white audiences. This, in turn, led to the opportunities for blues singers such as Bessie Smith to record and become celebrities in their own right.

"Crazy Blues" is a blues song with three different strains. Following a short instrumental introduction, the first part ("I can't sleep at night . . .") sets the tone of the spurned woman yearning for her unfaithful man. The next part ("There's a change in the ocean . . .") introduces a standard twelve-bar blues, although, as with the other blues sections in this song, the second line has a different text than the first. The third strain is similar to the first in that it has the contour of a popular stage song (AABA in sixteen bars) and functions as the refrain ("Now I've got the crazy blues . . ."), which returns to close out the recording after two more blues strains. The last of the blues sections uses a motif that was probably traditional in southern culture by that point and was to become an almost clichéd image in the blues lexicon:

> I went to the railroad, laid my head on the track
> I thought about my daddy and then I snatched it back
> Now my man's gone and gave me the sack

The final appearance of the B section prefigures the violent lyrics of rap singers eight decades later:

> I'm gonna do like a Chinaman,
> Get myself some hop,
> Get myself a gun and shoot myself a cop

Lyrics such as this would probably have earned a parental warning sticker in another time, as well as condemnation from law enforcement agencies and Asian groups. Themes that seem to advocate or celebrate violence have always been present in either direct or indirect ways in popular African American music, largely as a response to oppressive authority.

The multipart structure of "Crazy Blues" shows the influence of both Tin Pan Alley and the vestiges of the older ragtime form. It is the introduction of the twelve-bar sections and their folk-like themes that were such a radical departure, especially when sung by an African American singer. Although sales figures for recordings during this period are murky at best, some estimates suggest that as many as 75,000 copies of this disc were sold within a month of its release—an extraordinary success by any standard, but one that instantly proved that black audiences were poised to become significant consumers of the recording industry. The urban black audiences that bought this record in unprecedented numbers were largely products of the previous decade's Great Migration from the south, and hearing a singer such as Mamie Smith sing music that was at least in part familiar to them and part of their heritage was a sea change. The accompanying group was likewise a departure from the more polished, pit orchestra style of the group on Smith's first recording. Although the personnel is not completely identified, it is basically a jazz group of cornet (Johnny Dunn), trombone, clarinet, violin, and piano (played by Perry Bradford) inventing (as Bradford says in his autobiography) an accompaniment in the recording studio that used much counterpoint and collective improvisation in the style of groups associated with New Orleans.

BLUES QUEENS

Mamie Smith's success opened the floodgates. The subsequent recorded success of numerous African American women singers had a profound influence on popular music during the 1920s. An enormous number of blues and blues-influenced songs were composed, published, and recorded during the first half of the decade, although the vogue for the style had begun to run its course by the mid-1920s, and a gradual diminution of repertoire and recording frequency can be seen from that time. A short list of singers identified with the style who began to record following Mamie Smith's initial success includes Alberta Hunter, Eva Taylor, Laura Rucker, Mary Stafford, Ethel Waters, Trixie Smith, and many more, representing a full range of both inspiration and competence.

These singers had for the most part carved out their careers in the North, incorporating "sophisticated" musical elements (such as the use of jazz effects) and Tin Pan Alley songs into their acts. By 1923, however, these devices had begun to lose their novelty appeal when presented in the guise of a blues performance. A public—white as well as black— now thoroughly familiar with the blues (albeit in a watered-down form) had begun to tire of the clichés and superficial elements of the music. Still, the prevailing conservatism of the recording companies held that the more authentic and earthy blues of Ma Rainey or Bessie Smith were too coarse for the taste of the general public. This is graphically demonstrated by the fact that Bessie Smith was turned down by as many as four recording companies before being signed by Columbia in 1923. She was even rejected by Harry Pace, W. C. Handy's former partner and the director of Black Swan, the only black-owned recording company in New York. Ma Rainey was to spend her entire recording career with the small, Chicago-based race label Paramount, with its comparatively primitive technology and rather limited distribution. That Smith was able to get a recording contract with a major label and then to score a success large enough to warrant its being repeatedly renewed for eight years is unprecedented. The only other blues singer in this category to approach Bessie Smith's recording success was the unrelated Clara Smith, who also recorded for Columbia and even appeared in duet with Bessie on three sides.

The separation between the vaudeville or cabaret singers and the "authentic" blues singers is certainly not one of clear definition. Performers in the latter category (such as Bessie Smith and Ma Rainey), though identified as blues singers from comparatively early in their careers, did not depend exclusively on the blues for their livelihood. When traveling in tent shows throughout the South (usually during the summer months) these entertainers intermingled blues numbers with comedy skits, dance routines, and instrumental interludes, usually in the popular style of the day—ragtime until the early 1920s, jazz thereafter. These shows would travel throughout the Deep South, playing to rural audiences and catering to "country" tastes. In these places, the more subtle styles of the cabaret singers would not have communicated well. These audiences demanded a visceral, immediate form of theater in which the blues came to play an increasingly important role. By 1923, the trend had moved away from the theatrical blues style to a more "authentic" southern voice exemplified by Ma Rainey, Clara Smith, Victoria Spivey, Ida Cox, and especially Bessie Smith.

The blues as a popular style can be seen by a quick examination of the black press during the period. Contests were held to judge blues songs and to create lyrics based on certain themes as well as to judge between individual performers. The first "album" of popular (non-classical) music was released in 1924—OKeh's "Twelve Room House for

Blues" consisted of a housing for twelve 78 rpm discs with notations, artwork, and even autographs. Suggestions for recordings to be included for later purchase were made by African American publisher and composer Clarence Williams. The crossover between the blues and the jazzy dance band style of the period was constant, with jazz musicians picking up extra income by accompanying singers in the recording studio and occasionally on tour as well, creating a fertile ground of cross influence. Though white blues singers were rare at the time, white musicians frequently recorded popular blues numbers—one of Paul Whiteman's early hit recordings (although not blues in form) was the "Wang Wang Blues," recorded in 1920 and composed by his trumpeter Henry Busse. Early white jazz bands such as the Original Dixieland Jazz Band, the Original Memphis Five, the New Orleans Rhythm Kings, and others featured a significant proportion of blues in their recorded repertoire and adopted the style of their African American contemporaries in their interpretation.

The recordings examined in this chapter give some idea of the Classic Blues scene throughout the 1920s and also of the different substyles that emerged over the course of the decade. These substyles represent singers active in the North (primarily on the vaudeville and cabaret stages) and the South (tent shows, minstrel shows, and circuses) and provide an idea of what different sections of the public identified as blues at different points in the decade.

CLARENCE WILLIAMS

Clarence Williams (1893–1965) was an important if enigmatic figure in the history of early jazz and blues. Born just outside New Orleans, Williams was touring on the black vaudeville circuit by the time he was in his early teens. Known initially as a singer and comedian, he acquired sufficient piano skills to be able to accompany other singers and to write songs. By the late 1910s he had established himself as a music publisher in Chicago, relocating his business to New York early in the next decade. During this period he married singer Eva Taylor (whose real name was Irene Gibbons, 1895–1977) and promoted her career as well as acting as a talent scout and music director for OKeh records.

Taylor was a remarkably prolific stage actress and performer who recorded frequently with Williams's groups as well as other bands throughout the 1920s and 1930s. She was not a blues singer, but she performed much blues material on record and in person in her various shows (including with her husband in *Bottomland* on Broadway in 1927) and regular radio appearances. Although he was not important as a performer, Williams made a mark on the New York jazz scene as a businessman—he was responsible for many early classic recordings and published many songs that are now considered jazz standards (his authorship of many songs credited to him has been called into question). Williams continued his publishing successes through the 1930s and maintained a presence on the New York music scene. He sold his business in 1943 and lived in retirement until his death.

SANTA CLAUS BLUES

Williams was an excellent businessman and promoter during the 1920s and 1930s. Quick to identify new trends, he realized very early that blues was going to be an important part of popular music and published many compositions not only based on blues progressions, but also using "blues" in the title (and often having little else to do with the style). A tune such as "Santa Claus Blues" (OKeh 8254, recorded October 16, 1925) was obviously aimed at the holiday market and utilized the blues-related themes of sadness and loss, albeit with tongue firmly planted in cheek. Composed by the white songwriter Gus Kahn and bandleader Charley Straight, the recording by the Clarence Williams Trio is introduced by a short prelude featuring Louis Armstrong on cornet (the only horn player on the session) that would not be out of place on any more traditional blues record of the period. Armstrong imparts a gravitas to the performance that is difficult to describe; his passionate, muted playing takes its inspiration from the style of his primary mentor, Joe "King" Oliver. Oliver was known as a mute specialist who could create extraordinary vocalized effects on his cornet by manipulation of an arsenal of mutes that included metal inserts, hats, and a rubber plunger, which seems to be what Armstrong uses in this recording. The cornet solo that opens the record (backed only by Clarence Williams's piano and Buddy Christian's banjo) fades into discrete commentary behind the vocal once Eva Taylor enters, with the exception of the midpoint of the chorus, where Armstrong plays a solo break (over a sustained vocal harmony), the sheer emotion of which seems to cast the rest of the performance in an absurd light.

The tune itself consists of a verse and chorus that speaks of the narrator's lack of enthusiasm for the Christmas season due to his/her lack of a partner and the concurrent fact that "Santa Claus has lost my address." The thirty-two-bar chorus has some elements of the blues progression (at least in the first and third eight-measure sections). The solemn tempo allows for only one verse and chorus after the introduction, with Taylor's clear, declamatory singing muddied somewhat by the close harmony offered by Williams and singer Clarence Todd throughout most of it. Although the lyrics might suggest a sorrowful performance, another period recording by a slightly larger group (Clarence Williams's Blue Five) transforms it into a fast, "high steppin'" tune that would not have been out of place danced by a chorus line in a show. Featuring the same musicians as were on the slower recording, the fast version adds Buster Bailey on soprano saxophone and Charlie Irvis on trombone. Recordings by several other groups from the same time preserve the jaunty character that de-emphasizes the blues elements present on the slower trio version.

TRIXIE'S BLUES

One highly publicized blues contest was sponsored by the famous white dancer Irene Castle in New York on January 20, 1922. Held at the Manhattan Casino in Harlem, the evening's entertainment was focused on performances by several black female singers who had been performing in local vaudeville and minstrel reviews. By popular acclamation the winner was declared to be Trixie Smith (1895–1943) for her own song, "Trixie's Blues," which she performed with the noted pianist James P. Johnson. As a result of her victory, Smith was hired by Black Swan recording company to record it and another tune.

The Black Swan recording of "Trixie's Blues" (Black Swan 2039, January 1922) was recorded at the end of January 1922 and features the singer accompanied by what sounds like a theater orchestra of several horns (trumpet, trombone, clarinet, and saxophone are audible), piano, drums, and possibly flute and banjo. The musicians are clearly reading from a written orchestration, so perhaps the creation of an arrangement for the winning song was part of the prize awarded on January 20, although Smith's next four recordings on Black Swan, made in March and April 1922, feature a similar sounding band (in one case called "James P. Johnson's Harmony Eight") before she began using a looser sounding group designated her "Jazz Masters" or "Down Home Syncopators" that was apparently led by Black Swan's recording director, pianist Fletcher Henderson.

The song itself consists of a twelve-bar verse that is not in blues form, followed by six blues choruses (the third is followed by an instrumental repeat of the verse). The lyrics are a connected lament about a faithless man who stays out all night and lies to his woman. The verse sets the scene, with the singer already determined to end the relationship:

I'm going to leave this town today
Sweet mama [unintelligible] away
Because my man don't treat me right—he never comes home at night
He stays out all night long—that's why sweet mama sings this song

The narrative continues as the singer continues to describe her man's actions in cheating on her, but takes a turn in the fourth chorus (following the instrumental interlude), in which the listener learns more about the man in a racial context:

Now some like high yaller, but give me my black and brown
Now some like high yaller, but give me my black and brown
'Cause the black will stick by you when a yaller throws you down

The lyrics of this song stand out for their time. "Trixie's Blues" was certainly one of the first blues recordings to feature lyrics composed by a woman and delivered from a specifically female perspective—a significant preview of how the genre developed by the time Bessie Smith began recording. The level of personal involvement by the singer in her narrative had not been particularly important before this, but as the decade progressed and Classic Blues began to establish itself as a genre, the level of agency (often marked by the singer having a hand in the composition of at least part of her repertoire) increased and became a key component of the best singers.

DOWNHEARTED BLUES

"Downhearted Blues" (Paramount 12005, July 1922) was one of the most familiar songs of the Classic Blues era, due in large part to the phenomenal success of recordings made by Bessie Smith and the composer Alberta Hunter. Hunter (1895–1984) was an entertainer who had left her native Memphis as a teenager to try her luck at singing in the cabarets of Chicago, at that time one of the centers of black entertainment. She found success as a singer and dancer in some of high-class nightspots in the city, including the Dreamland Cafe, where she was featured singing with a band led by New Orleans cornetist King Oliver in 1921 and 1922. It was at this time that she collaborated with pianist Lovie Austin on the song that gave her a hit recording for Paramount records in July 1922.

Hunter is accompanied on this recording session by a well-rehearsed studio band that some have speculated might have been led by African American composer and pianist Eubie Blake, who was at the time leading the pit orchestra for his show *Shuffle Along*. If this is the case, the piano is inaudible and the band seems to be playing from a published stock arrangement that allows for little or no improvisation. Even the instrumental breaks at the end of the second line of each blues chorus (played in order by saxophone, clarinet, trombone, cornet, and saxophone again) are, with exception of the cornet break, identical and obviously written out. The arranged horn parts are for at least the four instruments mentioned, with others possibly in the mix, as well—the dull recorded sound makes it difficult to tell. There seems to be a tuba, some light percussion, and presumably a piano and/or banjo as well, giving a theatrical flair to the arrangement by the precise intonation and articulation not often found in blues or jazz recordings of a slightly later period.

Beginning with an instrumental introduction followed by a non-blues verse ("Gee, but it's hard to love someone when that someone don't love you"), the tune quickly moves into the main event—five blues choruses tracing the trajectory of a failed romance through self-affirmation and ultimately triumph in the iconic imagery of the final chorus:

> I've got the world in a jug and the stopper in my hand
> I've got the world in a jug and the stopper in my hand

And if you want me pretty papa you gotta come under my command

Though this recording features very little of the freewheeling quality of many later Classic Blues performances, it represents the blues as a theatrical presentation—when Handy's blues of the middle 1910s became popular hits, many Broadway and vaudeville performers began presenting them in their shows and revues. Alberta Hunter had considerably more exposure to the southern blues tradition than did many cabaret singers, and her performance here can be heard as a triumph over the accompaniment in its flexible approach. She conveys emotion to the theatrical text not by melodramatic presentation, but instead with blues elements such as wails, moans, bent (or blue) notes, as well as vocal ornamentation. Her wailing introduction of the fourth chorus ("Now it may be a week, it may be a month or two") is especially effective when heard against the static accompaniment and even energizes the group, which momentarily seems to begin to catch the spirit. The fact that Hunter herself wrote the lyrics (assisted by Austin) further expresses the point that these blues singers were beginning to be valued not just for their performance, but for their perspective as well.

BOLL WEAVIL BLUES

Ma Rainey was born Gertrude Pridgett in Columbus, Georgia, in 1886 and was working in the theater by the time she was in her early teens. In 1904 she married William "Pa" Rainey and the two of them toured with numerous vaudeville, tent show, and circus troupes until his death in 1919. Following that, she toured as a single before retiring in the early 1930s. Rainey recalled hearing blues as early as 1902, soon after adding them to her repertoire and becoming known in the process as one of the first blues singers. Sometime around 1914, the Raineys and a very young Bessie Smith were in the same company (perhaps the Tolliver Circus and Tent Show or the Rabbit Foot Minstrels) and it is speculated that Smith was influenced by the older Rainey. With a career reaching back to the beginning years of the century, Ma Rainey was even closer to the indigenous southern blues tradition than was Smith. Her base of popularity rested squarely in the Deep South, with few people in the North even being aware of her existence before she began making records. Ma Rainey, then, serves as a link between the blues as a rural folk music and the blues as first a popular music and then later an art form.

This immediate connection to the earlier tradition is most evident in Rainey's accompaniment on records. Though Smith probably had little or no control over her accompanying groups in the studio (a topic discussed later), Rainey evidently had some input, even to the extent of sometimes using her touring group. A comparison of her studio groups with those on record with Bessie Smith shows a decided preference for the more "common" or "vernacular" elements of southern folk music, such as jug bands and musical saws, which were designed to appeal to rural southern audiences. Smith was also accompanied by such devices on occasion (country fiddle players, for example), but her groups were uniformly more "modern." This is in part explained by the differences in the two singers' target audiences. For her entire career Smith made records for the nationally known and distributed Columbia label. Rainey, on the other hand, recorded in Chicago for the small Paramount label, which was by definition a "race" label—a designation invented when the popularity of black popular music among African Americans became known (although other races and ethnicities were likewise targeted by marketing devices). Even large companies such as Columbia had separate catalog entries in a numeric series that were designed specifically for various racial groups. A small company such as Paramount owed much of what there was of its national distribution either to mail order business or to agents such as Pullman porters, who would take large quantities of their records to distant locations (mostly in the South) and sell them at a profit to black communities that had heard the artists in person.

This folk influence is not in evidence in the accompaniment of "Boll Weavil Blues," Rainey's own composition, which comes from her first recording session (Paramount 12080, December 1923). Backed by pianist Lovie Austin (one of the most widely respected female instrumentalists of the 1920s and co-composer of "Downhearted Blues"), New Orleans cornetist Tommy Ladnier, and Chicago clarinetist Jimmy O'Bryant, Rainey benefits from a trio of musicians who were completely at home with blues expression and improvising blues accompaniment. She herself sings with a world-weary quality that earned her the marketing title "queen of the moaners" and represents a tradition of African American singing in the South that probably reached back before the turn of the century, as is suggested by the title of the song, which celebrates the scourge of the southern cotton crop.

After a short instrumental introduction, Rainey sings four blues choruses at a stately tempo, which, although not significantly slower, seem dirge-like compared to "Crazy Blues" with its breezier approach. The first three choruses are fairly standard in their use of text, but Rainey organizes her phrases in unorthodox ways, creating accents and syllabic patterns that are unexpected but quite beguiling. The third stanza sums up the love lament:

> I don't want no man to put no sugar in my tea
> I don't want no man to put no sugar in my tea
> Some men are so evil, I'm afraid they might poison me

The final vocal chorus is in fact only eight bars of what theatrically was called a "patter"—a text-driven section that can be equated with operatic recitative and ends with explicit "looked at my bed—gettin' tired of sleeping by myself," which represents another step toward the agency of the performer beyond the simple expressions of a popular song. The eight bars of this patter (words) turn out to be the first two lines of the blues form, which are then succeeded by an instrumental turn on the last four bars and then a short coda.

There exist two takes of "Boll Weavil Blues" from this session. The second is a bit faster, and the increase in speed sacrifices a certain amount of the darker quality of the first take, although they both have the same sequence of stanzas and general feeling. Rainey again recorded the song at one of her last sessions in 1927 at an even slower tempo and with a slightly larger backing group but with exactly the same arrangement, suggesting that her performance on record was recreated from her stage presentation or vice versa.

KISS ME SWEET

Jodie Edwards (1895–1967) began his show business career as a teenager singing in various tent and variety shows during the 1910s. In 1917 he met and married Susie Hawthorne (1896–1963) during a run of the *Smart Set* touring company, and by the early 1920s they were performing as Butterbeans and Susie, perfecting the husband-and-wife act that carried them to consistent if not extravagant success on the Theatre Owner's Booking Agents (TOBA) tours throughout the decade. Their stage presence depended on the time-tested roles of battling spouses, translated through the prism of an African American cultural sensibility. Their act featured comedy sketches, duo numbers, and dance routines, although Susie would also sing blues as part of each show. Their recording career during the 1920s and 1930s preserved some of their most successful blues and novelty numbers.

Male/female acts of this sort were a staple on the tent show and vaudeville circuit during the time that Bessie Smith was living the life of a touring vaudevillian. Smith herself toured for a year with male singer and dancer Wayne "Buzzin' Burton around 1913 and received some of her first positive press attention through the association. These acts invariably combined singing, dancing, and comedy that capitalized on husband/wife relations as viewed through African American experience, although understandable to everyone at its most elemental level.

"Kiss Me Sweet," (OKeh 8182, September 12, 1924) by the New Orleans violinist and bandleader Armand Piron and pianist Steve Lewis, perfectly fits the style of Butterbeans and Susie. Though not mining the racy humor for which they were sometimes noted (one song they recorded that was initially held back by Okeh was "I Wanna Hot Dog for My Roll," a gold mine of sexual double entendre), this tune matched their stage roles as an antagonistic but usually loving married couple. Accompanied by pianist Clarence Williams and cornetist Joe "King" Oliver (both natives of New Orleans), the couple trades verses of this pop tune with frequent blues inflections before combining on the chorus, playing up the banter implied in the lyrics:

> [Susie] Kiss me now, I can't wait no longer, seems somehow my love is growing stronger
> You growing old, I've known you for years,
> [Jodie] I can still climb a hill without shifting a gear
> [Susie] My love ain't complete honey till you kiss me sweet

Butterbeans and Susie had a remarkably durable marriage and act, lasting more than forty years. For much of that time they served as mentors to younger black entertainers while touring ceaselessly on the various tent show and vaudeville circuits around the country.

DINAH

Ethel Waters (1896–1977) was perhaps the most successful singer identified with Classic Blues in a long-term sense. After a difficult and
unsettled childhood, she began singing as a teenager and touring on the
black vaudeville and circus circuits. By 1919 she had moved to New
York, where she established a reputation as a blues singer (nicknamed
"Sweet Mama Stringbean") as well as singer of popular songs. By the
1930s she had transitioned into a star of Broadway and on film, making
recordings of sophisticated popular songs. The television era found her
starring in the early sitcom *Beulah* in 1951 and making frequent guest
appearances on other shows. She ended her long career singing with
the Billy Graham crusade in the 1960s and 1970s.

Waters's career in the 1920s involved vaudeville tours, stage shows,
frequent recordings, and even film appearances at the end of the
decade. She was among the first African American women to record,
making her first session in 1921 for the Cardinal label and then signing
with Black Swan, where she recorded a number of blues hits, which
caused Bessie Smith to view her as competition (Waters, 1967, 90–91).
After Black Swan went bankrupt at the end of 1923, she signed with
Columbia, recording with them until 1931, ending three months before
Smith's last session for that company. During this period, Waters's recordings were initially released in Columbia's general catalog, but by
the end of 1925 most were issued on the 14000, "race" series (see
chapter 3). By 1929 she was again part of the main catalog, clearly
illustrating the evolution of her style toward an audience that was primarily white.

Perhaps the biggest recorded success Waters had in the 1920s was of
a new popular song, "Dinah" (Columbia 487-D, October 20, 1925).
Composed by Harry Akst, Sam Lewis, and Joe Young for Waters's show
The New Plantation Revue, "Dinah" became one of the hits of the
decade, using the modern Tin Pan Alley form of a short verse followed
by a thirty-two bar AABA chorus. Waters is here accompanied by the
orchestra from the show—an African American group playing from
what is obviously a theatrical orchestration. Her singing is a combination of intimacy and power, demonstrating what made her stand out
from her contemporaries at the time. Her trilled *r*'s and exacting pro-
nunciation locate this performance firmly in the theatrical tradition,

although in the second chorus she begins taking liberties with the melody, improvising as a jazz musician would. Her flexible and expressive
voice clearly has elements of blues singing in it, especially the last eight
bars, in which she makes liberal use of blue notes. From this point,
Waters's career was irreversibly directed to theatrical presentations,
most often for white audiences.

2

MAMA'S GOT THE BLUES

The business of "show business" for black performers in the first decades of the twentieth century was a complex gumbo of styles and influences that was, as has always been the case in the entertainment industry, dependent on the audience. When Bessie Smith began her professional career, black entertainment was in a state of transition. The late 1880s had seen the rise of the black minstrel show—though not a strict copy of the traditional white minstrel programs that had been around since well before the Civil War, these black shows used a similar structure but lampooned the dominant white establishment as well as introducing some of its own vernacular music. The next step toward independence of expression was through the circuses. Traveling circuses had become staples on the American scene by the 1890s, and many of them included African American entertainers in their troupes. Although rarely invited to perform with the main acts under the big top, the black bands and singers effectively constituted their own circus that enlivened the "sideshow"—the simultaneously running acts outside the main venue. These groups were also featured parts of the parades held to publicize the arrival of a circus in a new location and as such catered to the popular taste of their audience. According to Lynn Abbott and Doug Seroff, these circuses and the tent shows that ultimately replaced them were integral to bringing black music (particularly the blues) to far-flung audiences (Abbott and Seroff 2002, 7).

The popularity of the circus sideshow bands encouraged African American producers and entertainers to put together revues that featured a wide range of performers, including singers, dancers, comics, and acrobats. Two concurrent strains of this type of show were those that played in established black vaudeville houses (located mostly in cities and larger towns) and tent shows, which essentially carried their own canvas theater with them. These tent shows would usually travel to remote parts of the South during the summer and fall (following the harvest season, when agricultural workers had money to spend and the desire for entertainment) and present a program something like the traditional minstrel show, but with more up-to-date acts—coon songs and blues or jazz, depending on the time period. As the shows developed over time, the connection to traditional minstrelsy faded, with the entertainers eventually rejecting its trappings (especially blackface makeup and demeaning vocabulary) entirely. These entertainers attempted to connect with their mostly black audiences by using elements of their shared culture, including humor and general delivery.

When the harvest season was over, many of the headlining acts of the tent shows transitioned to theatrical revues on the vaudeville circuit. These revues were similar to the tent shows in that they presented a variety of entertainment, but they had a more urban flavor, striving for more sophistication of humor, music, and presentation. At their highest level, these shows often rivaled Broadway productions—noted black entertainers of this period including Ernest Hogan, Bert Williams, George Walker, and Bob Cole had all begun in traditional minstrelsy but evolved their acts and developed their followings to the point where they could mount large-scale shows that were occasionally presented on Broadway. Although these shows (mostly done before 1910) featured syncopated music and coon songs inspired by the ragtime era, they did not present anything along the lines of blues, which was considered too common for a high-class show of the time.

The musical variety that was presented by these shows was dependent to a degree on the level of sophistication or the racial component of its audience. Circuses (even the sideshows) were performed for both white and black audiences in towns of all sizes, featuring music that ran the gamut from Sousa marches and arrangements of operatic selections, to currently popular Tin Pan Alley tunes, and eventually to blues and folk music as well. The theatrical shows leaned much more heavily on contemporary Tin Pan Alley fare and any currently fashionable dances (cakewalks, foxtrots, etc.) designed to appeal to urban black audiences.

Tent shows were primarily for the country folk and, although using popular tunes of the day, leavened their fare with accessible music and humor that leaned toward vernacular expression in which blues, folk, and even pseudo-religious music were vital components. Though Bessie Smith apparently did not have significant experience touring with circus companies, she alternated between tent shows and stage revues for more than a decade before her recording career made her a celebrity on a national scale.

Beginning in 1909 with a non-featured role in the chorus line of the Moses Stokes revue, Smith gradually learned the ropes of the African American entertainment industry through a succession of associations with casual and established shows. After some modest success as part of a male/female comedy duo with Wayne "Buzzin" Burton from 1913 to 1914, Smith was given more featured numbers in various shows, receiving good reviews and significant press attention for her work with the Florida Blossoms show in 1916 (Abbott and Seroff 2002, 299). It was here that she was specifically commended for her work singing blues, including W. C. Handy's "Hesitation Blues," "St. Louis Blues," and "Yellow Dog Blues," recording the latter two a decade later. At this time, black singers (especially females) were often referred to in the black press as "up to date coon shouters," both affirming and undermining the popular concept of a "coon shouter" as a white woman singer, the most popular examples of which were Sophie Tucker and May Irwin. By 1916, however, African American women singing in this style and with this repertoire were beginning to be credited as "blues singers," and most of the traveling tent shows included at least one such performer.

These popular blues numbers were by no means the only songs a blues singer might sing in one of these shows. Popular and novelty songs were demanded, as was the ability to dance and perform comedy skits that might draw on various aspects of the African American experience. Male/female relations were, then as now, a font of varying degrees of inspiration, with Smith and Burton being just one example. More popular was the husband-and-wife team of Butterbeans and Susie (discussed in chapter 1), which toured various black entertainment circuits and made frequent recordings from the early 1920s until 1960.

After the summer tent show season, singers such as Smith and Ma Rainey returned to their home bases (Rainey to Chicago and Smith to

New York and Philadelphia) and began rehearsing a variety show or revue for a fall tour on the Theatre Owner's Booking Agents vaudeville circuit, known as TOBA (referred to by performers as "tough on black artists/asses"). These shows featured more sophisticated, urban entertainment than did the tent shows. Entertainers traveling on the TOBA circuit, which was organized in 1920 around a loose affiliation of black theaters throughout the country, received much exposure and subsequently enabled them to sell thousands of records.

The repertoire sung by these established "blues" singers ran the gamut of popular music of the day. Bessie Smith was called on to sing far more than the blues, for which she is justly acclaimed. Fortunately, she was able to record a number of other selections that might have been part of her early repertoire, at least stylistically. Accounts of her later career as well as her later recordings give further evidence that she continually updated her playlist with pop tunes and novelties in an effort to please an ever-changing audience.

The first two examples discussed here come from one recording session made on March 2, 1927. This session produced four tunes that were obviously intended to cover the "popular" market, even though they were released on the 14000-D "race" series. One current song ("Muddy Water") and three chestnuts—"After You've Gone" (1918), "There'll Be a Hot Time in the Old Town Tonight" (1896), and "Alexander's Ragtime Band" (1911)—were recorded. The backing group was a Dixieland-style group of cornet, trombone, clarinet, piano, and banjo, with a second clarinet added on "Muddy Water." The musicians were all members of the band—led by pianist Fletcher Henderson—that was currently in residence at the Roseland Ballroom in New York City. This group was considered the greatest African American band of its day and was celebrated for its innovations in dance music as well as for its musicianship and jazz playing. The full band was twelve members, but the Blue Boys consisted of just five or six—the piano (Henderson), banjo (Charlie Dixon), and the main soloists of the big band: Joe Smith on cornet, Jimmy Harrison on trombone, and Coleman Hawkins and/or Buster Bailey on clarinet. Though probably not intended to do so, this session represents an interesting snapshot of the type and range of music Smith might have been performing as part of her tours during the 1910s with a minstrel tune, a popular "ragtime" number, a jazzier "pop" tune, and one selection with blues associations included.

THERE'LL BE A HOT TIME IN THE OLD TOWN TONIGHT

This song is the oldest published tune recorded by Bessie Smith. Composed in 1896 by Theodore Metz specifically for use in the parade that heralded the arrival of minstrel companies in small towns throughout the country, "There'll Be a Hot Time in the Old Town Tonight" (Columbia 14219-D, March 2, 1927) has lyrics by Joe Hayden that call to mind camp meetings and stylized African American social gatherings of the nineteenth century. Metz led the band for the McIntyre and Heath Minstrels, a white company that was one of the most popular groups in the genre from 1874 to 1924, and this song became a significant national hit, abetted by the fact that it became known as the rallying song for Teddy Roosevelt's Rough Riders during the Spanish American War.

The tune itself is made up of the verse and chorus. During these early years of Tin Pan Alley, the verse was generally the part of the song that drove the narrative, with the chorus (sometimes called the refrain) functioning as the "sing-along" part, which encouraged audience participation. In this tune, the two sections elide, with the lyrics of the refrain changing in part on the repeat. The Bessie Smith recording is further complicated by key adjustments, presumably to deal with issues of vocal range.

Perhaps the least "jazzy" of any of the tunes recorded that day, "Hot Time" features an accompaniment that sounds as if it could have been played under canvas during the early 1900s. With an overwhelmingly ragtime feel, the group seems only to be embellishing, rather than improvising; even Buster Bailey's flashy solo clarinet break in the middle of the instrumental chorus is more of a technical display than a musical statement. It is not difficult to hear this—as with "Alexander's Ragtime Band"—as a nostalgic evocation of the musical landscape of rural black entertainment from a generation before this recording was made.

For her part, Smith overcomes the novelty and stereotypical elements of the song even as she evokes the earlier time. Her experiences doing shows similar to those done by the McIntyre and Heath minstrels (albeit with black casts for black audiences) must certainly have included this tune and many of similar provenance. The arrangement of the song is curious; whereas the original version is harmonically static with diatonic chords, Smith (and probably Henderson) have included several modulations in this version, perhaps to adjust for some issues of vocal range but also maybe to give some harmonic and tonal variety to the performance.

Her insistence on singing "There's a Hot Time in Old Town To-night" with the elimination of the final article in the title suggests the original version of the song, which was apparently inspired by a visit to a location known as "Old Town"; one wonders if this was something she learned closer to the source than the published sheet music. Her impo-sition of cultural and racial codes (blue notes, moans, growls, verbal interpolations) were probably no different in 1927 than they had been in 1917, and the deliberately conservative accompaniment highlights this connection as well.

ALEXANDER'S RAGTIME BAND

One of the first great Tin Pan Alley successes of the twentieth century was "Alexander's Ragtime Band" (Columbia 14219-D, March 2, 1927), a song composed by Irving Berlin and published by Ted Snyder in 1911. Though not Berlin's first published song, it was his first hit; after a slow beginning, the song took off, largely due to good placement in traveling reviews, where it was performed by popular singers such as Emma Carus, Billy Murray, and Al Jolson. "Alexander" occupies a tran-sitional period in the history of the American Songbook, with roots in the coon songs of the late nineteenth and early decades of the twentieth century. The lyrics as published make use of some racial stereotypes (although the picture on the original sheet music edition features a white band) and dialect ("it's just the bestest band what am, my honey lamb"). The title also references popular music that originated in the African American community and that was already moving past its peak by 1911.

Nevertheless, "Alexander's Ragtime Band" became enormously pop-ular and widely influential with its uncommon structure, wide vocal range, and syncopated melody, which, though not ragtime, evoked that tradition. The punchy melody of the chorus incorporates a stylized bu-gle call, both a quote from and a lyrical reference to Stephen Foster's iconic 1851 song "Old Folks at Home" (also known as "Swanee River"), and a surprising internal deceptive cadence. Many recordings of the tune were even made in Europe during the 1910s—apparently its qualities somehow signified positive aspects of the American experience across the globe.

When Bessie Smith began her career at the 81 Club in Atlanta in 1912, Berlin's song was among the hottest properties in shows, reviews, and at dances. Smith would surely have been familiar with it at the time and probably danced to its strains while she was in the chorus line of the Stokes troupe and at the 81 Theater. By 1927 "Alexander" had already achieved legendary status and enjoyed a brief resurgence, possibly in connection with the republication of the sheet music. In the early months of that year, the song was recorded by numerous bands and entertainers, including clarinetist Jimmy Lytell, trombonist Miff Mole (featuring cornetist Red Nichols), and comedian and clarinetist Ted Lewis. On March 2, Bessie Smith recorded it, accompanied by "Her Blue Boys" (Columbia 14219-D).

Beginning with a short instrumental introduction, the recording goes directly into the first verse (the second is not sung on this record) and then the chorus. For anyone familiar with the original version of the song, the quality of Smith's voice is striking in the way it changes the character of the tune. Instead of a nostalgic evocation of the palmy days of band concerts and antebellum leisure, a gritty, bluesy interpretation presents an alternate image. It is not too romantic a notion to hear Smith's shouting presentation as a look back into a tent show performance of "Alexander" in the Deep South of the previous decade. After this, the band plays a loosely improvised chorus in the Dixieland style with Joe Smith's rich-toned cornet prominent both in the ensemble and the solo break in the middle. The singer then returns to sing another chorus, encouraging the band with moans and shouts that come from the gospel tradition as much as the blues. By using these elements of African American vernacular music, Bessie Smith effectively returns Irving Berlin's song to its root culture, albeit in a different way than that which inspired the composer in the first place.

YELLOW DOG BLUES

Sometimes the mark of genius is being in the right place at the right time and being aware enough to take advantage of the situation. So it was with W. C. Handy (1873–1958), who learned music as a way of escaping the rural Alabama poverty into which he was born. Largely self-taught, he nevertheless learned enough music theory and note reading to begin a career teaching music and directing bands by the time he was in his early twenties. By the late 1890s he was touring the South as both a singer and cornet player. As the latter he took over management and direction of Mahara's Minstrels, which toured continuously for three years until 1899, when he was hired to teach music at an agricultural college in Alabama. In 1902, he rejoined Mahara and traveled with them again through the South and as far as the West Coast and Pacific Northwest (he had been to Cuba during his first tour). It was during this period that Handy acknowledged being exposed to a peculiarly black style of folk music that he later identified as blues.

By 1909 he was leading what came to be known as "Handy's Band," using Memphis as his base of operations. While in Memphis, Handy began to compose music for his group, intending to capture elements of the folk music he had been hearing in notation. His first piece was "The Memphis Blues," which he published as an instrumental before selling the rights to Theron Bennett for a flat $100. Bennett took the song to New York and pushed it relentlessly, having it recorded numerous times and included in the act of dancers Vernon and Irene Castle, who used it to accompany their new fox-trot dance step (accompanied by the African American bandleader James Reese Europe). Shortly after this, Handy joined forces with black businessman Harry Pace to found Pace and Handy Sheet Music, which published his songs thereafter.

In 1917 Handy and Pace moved their operation to New York and joined the crowd of music publishers vying to have popular entertainers perform and record their pieces. As the only African American music publishing company in the city, they felt that black musicians would be supportive of their efforts. This turned out to be far too optimistic, as was Pace's decision to leave the company early in 1921 to found an all-black recording company called Black Swan. Although the music recorded by this label was generally high quality, sales were meager. The white companies' dominance of the industry was largely responsible, though Pace's initial reluctance to record popular music was also a factor, and Black Swan went out of business in less than two years. Handy also dealt with business reversals, almost going bankrupt in 1921 and temporarily losing his sight. Both his sight and solvency returned later in the decade when several of his songs began to generate revenue, in part based on the popular recordings done by Bessie Smith.

One of the many tunes Handy published during his time in Memphis was "Yellow Dog Rag" in 1915, a blues tune that was a follow-up to a popular number of two years earlier called "I Wonder Where My Easy Rider's Gone" by Shelton Brooks. Moderately successful at best, "Yellow Dog Rag" was rechristened "Yellow Dog Blues" in 1919 and immediately found popularity via its Victor recording by the white society band led by Joseph C. Smith. Consisting of only two strains (the second in the subdominant key), this tune is one of Handy's most simple blues, telling the story of Susan Johnson, whose man had disappeared, and her efforts to track him down. In the second strain she finds out that he has been riding the rails and ended up "where the Southern cross the Yellow Dog," a reference to the junction of the Southern Railway and Yazoo Delta Railroad in Mississippi.

Bessie Smith recorded "Yellow Dog Blues" (Columbia 14075-D, May 6, 1925) with a group of musicians drawn from the Fletcher Henderson Orchestra, this time credited as "Henderson's Hot Six." This tune was part of Columbia's initial series of experiments with the new electrical recording system, which was to replace the traditional acoustic method. In this, the sounds were captured by an electrical component system using microphones rather than the more primitive way of having the musicians gather around a series of horns, making acoustical balance and fidelity largely a matter of chance. Both "Yellow Dog" and "Cake Walking Babies" (recorded the previous day, to be discussed in chapter 4) were ambitious undertakings not only for the new process, but for having Smith record with the largest band she had used so far in studio. Apparently, the band, singer, and several technicians were clustered together under a small tent in order to keep extraneous sounds out—an uncomfortable situation to be sure that was probably the main reason only one tune was cut each day.

Compared to Smith's previous recordings, the sound of "Yellow Dog Blues" represents a dramatic shift—now, her voice comes through with much more clarity and precision, as do the instruments behind her. Joe Smith's cornet is the main beneficiary of the sound separation, and it might be the fact that he was regarded as a technical and highly sophisticated player that he was hired to do the session in place of his section mate in the Henderson band, Louis Armstrong. Although Armstrong had been Smith's primary cornet accompanist on her earlier sessions, his legendary volume and tonal intensity may have been perceived as being too much for the new technology; however, he returned for several classic recordings later in the spring. A comparison of the Bessie Smith tunes recorded during these two days with two tunes made by Maggie Jones at the same time (and with the same group) shows that Columbia's engineers were still in an experimental phase. The Jones sides are extremely clear and sound much more technically advanced than those by Smith. Fortunately, the various kinks were worked out by the next sessions.

"Yellow Dog Blues" is one of the few songs in Bessie Smith's discography that exists in two takes. Both the master (take one, which may not have been the first take recorded) and the second take were released for some reason, but the existence of both allows the listener to get a glimpse of Smith's recording habits. The routine is exactly the same: after an eight-measure instrumental introduction that references the melody of the chorus (and played virtually note for note on each take, suggesting it was written out at least in part), Smith sings the three choruses of the first (verse) strain and then the two choruses of the second (chorus). Generally, the horns remain discretely in the background, with usually one at a time putting in fills at the end of the vocal lines. The primary take is a bit livelier and has more of a sense of order than does the second, which is considerably slower—the take lasts an additional thirteen seconds—and was probably the lesser of the two due to the disagreement of tempo between the introduction and the vocal entrance. In general, the second take has an earthier feel, with Smith projecting the moaning, dark qualities associated with Ma Rainey more than on practically any of her other recordings.

For the most part, Smith sings Handy's published lyrics, taking liberties with the melody occasionally and of course imparting much more of the blues style than could be reproduced by musical notation. Whereas Handy wrote, "Everywhere that Uncle Sam has even a rural delivery," in reference to Susan Johnson's letters asking for the whereabouts of her man, Smith sings the much more evocative (and poetic), "Everywhere that Uncle Sam is the ruler of delivery," which some singers still use to this day. The newfound clarity in the sound spectrum makes the listener realize the power of Smith's voice in relation to the instruments and how she could musically dominate the proceedings, even to the point of altering tempo.

MOAN YOU MOANERS

One of the defining elements of African American popular culture in the twentieth century was gospel music. As an outgrowth of Protestant hymnody, black spirituals, and jubilee songs, gospel evolved into a recognizable form by the late 1920s, concurrent with the rise of jazz. Chief among its founders was pianist and composer Thomas A. Dorsey (1899–1993), who grew up in Atlanta surrounded by church music but was pulled toward popular theatrical music. The presence of religious performance practice was never far from the surface in any aspect of black entertainment at the time, and the tension that existed between secular and sacred performance was an integral part of the scene. So too did tension exist between traditional and "new" practices, both in religious and stage performance, with the older style being marked by emotionalism and generally untutored expression, while the newer was more urban influenced and comparatively detached in its performance. Nevertheless, performance practice was a fluid thing, and the old and new methods were usually blended to varying degrees depending on the audience. For his part, Dorsey developed a new type of religious music from his experiences listening to theatrical shows at the 81 Theater and performing as a pianist, first in local jazz groups and then as the touring musical director for Ma Rainey. This new blended style came to be known as gospel.

As a boy, Dorsey sold refreshments at the 81 Theater in the African American district of Atlanta, where he became familiar with the black entertainers who regularly played there, including Ma Rainey and Bessie Smith. Smith began performing in shows there in 1912 and 1913 as a dancer and occasional singer. She participated as a contract player in revues there and in several other theaters in the South owned by the same corporation for, at first, $10 per week, although the real benefit was in the immersion in all aspects of show business (Scott 2008, 116–17). During the 1910s, Atlanta was home to a thriving blues scene that saw Smith, Rainey, Dorsey, and later famous male singers like Barbecue Bob, Blind Willie McTell, and Buddy Moss using the city as their home base. Smith was known in these early days as primarily a dancer and comic, participating in the standard husband-and-wife skits popular in African American theater. The theatrical aspect of nascent gospel music was mirrored by Classic Blues, both being inseparable from their roots in black vaudeville, circus, and tent shows. It was on these circuits that a performer like Bessie Smith cut her teeth as singer, dancer, and comic, a combination of versatility and a concentration on theatrical presentation that is discussed by Paige McGinley (2014).

"Moan You Moaners" was a faux-gospel song composed by the New Orleans pianist and entertainer Spencer Williams apparently in 1930 but not published until 1931. The recording of the tune by Bessie Smith was done before the actual publication by Joe Davis Inc., and the record label credits the title as "Moan Mourners," which might suggest that Williams had used that as its original title before the formal publication, although that phrase does not appear in the lyrics. The version by Fletcher Henderson and His Orchestra as well as recordings by Red Nichols and Gus Arnheim were made either immediately before or following the copyright date of the sheet music and use the more familiar title.

Bessie Smith's recording (Columbia 14538-D, June 9, 1930) highlights both the church-influenced atmosphere of the song's inspiration as well as the comedy potential of lampooning the earnestness of a country preacher. This trope of African American entertainment was a vital part of the industry during the minstrel and vaudeville period and continues to this day. Other period examples on record include Louis Armstrong's "Lonesome Road" (OKeh 41538, 1931) and his 1938 "Elder Eatmore" sermons, which were in turn re-creations of 1919 records by the great black entertainer, Bert Williams. One of the most prolific black recording artists of the Depression era was Reverend J. M. Gates, whose sermons (sometimes with musical accompaniment) were widely popular among African Americans. In common with many Pentecostal preachers of the day, Gates used a highly charged and fulsome delivery that was ripe for parody (one of his most popular sides was "Death Might Be Your Santa Claus") and Bessie Smith's recording of "Moan You Moaners" would have been a familiar treatment of the sacred side of black life as seen from the stage.

Smith's accompaniment on this record and its flip side, "On Revival Day," is the great Harlem stride pianist James P. Johnson and the Bessemer Singers. This group was a gospel quartet from Birmingham, Alabama, and their career illustrates the complicated relationship between secular and sacred music in the African American community at the time. Originally called the Dunham Jazz and Jubilee Singers, their career took them touring throughout the 1920s and recording several times before the Bessie Smith session. As the Dunham Jubilee Singers, they recorded gospel numbers; as the Dunham Jazz Singers, they did blues songs; and as the Bessemer Quartette, they were responsible for minstrel-influenced material like "Can't You Hear Those Darkies Singing?" It is possible that such deception was intentional in order to draw a distinct line between the different styles of (and audiences for) the music. Their contribution to "On Revival Day" and "Moan You Moaners" is primarily to give a vocal cushion to Smith's shouting on the former and preaching on the latter. For the most part, they just hum chords in the background with an occasional arranged response to simulate a gospel service.

Beginning with a section of comic "preaching" over harmonized moaning by the vocal group, Smith demonstrates the skills that encouraged Columbia to credit her as "comedienne" on her first record releases. After the tempo is established by Johnson, Smith sings the minor keyed and theatrical verse with some responses by the group. The chorus (in typical Tin Pan Alley AABA form rather than the less complicated structure of most spirituals or gospel tunes) is sung through twice, the second time involving more pitch manipulations and growl effects on the part of the singer. Smith is in good voice on this, one of her last sessions: at the end of "On Revival Day" she even climaxes on a high E flat at the very top of her vocal range, an unusual reach for her at any point in her recording career.

Why Smith was compelled to record these two quasi-religious pieces with a gospel group is something of a mystery. It might have been an attempt by Columbia to reenergize her recording career, which, in common with most of her contemporaries, was seriously flagging by 1930 due to the Depression and changing tastes. In any event, it obviously was not a successful enough experiment to warrant repeating, although the results give a fascinating glimpse of a popular entertainer's take on a parallel strain of black vernacular experience and a reflection of her own upbringing and performance influences.

CARELESS LOVE

The song "Careless Love" probably predates the blues. It was apparently a folk song that goes back at least to the 1880s but may have antecedents well before that (Courlander 1992, 138–39). Though not blues in structure, the song has some lyrical similarities with the form, including a repeating initial line ("Love oh love, oh careless love") that functions as a refrain. With a sixteen-bar structure, it also has elements of a folk ballad from the earlier Anglo-American tradition. As with many such folk melodies, both black and white audiences claimed it for their own. W. C. Handy co-opted the tune, added lyrics, and published it as "Loveless Love" in 1921. The lyrics sung by Bessie Smith express a self-reflexive lament about the poor choices the singer has made in love, a state that Smith surely viewed as autobiographical at the time of her recording (Columbia 14083-D, May 26, 1925), given her tumultuous relationship with Jack Gee, whom she married in 1923. Although the marriage lasted through the decade (they may never have officially divorced), the association was characterized by frequent violence, cheating, separations, and strife over the care of their adopted son.

This song, or an adaptation of it, was recorded by blues singers in the 1920s perhaps more than any other, except "St. Louis Blues." Bessie Smith's recording (which exists in two takes) seems to take a more traditional view of the lyrics, which utilize a syntax quite different from any of her other recordings. Some of the expressions seem more akin to the Old English still used by white rural communities in the early 1900s than the black vernacular speech we associate with Smith and the other Classic Blues singers. The recording of "Careless Love" by the country (then called "hillbilly") singer Lulu Jackson is in fact closer to Smith's conception than, for example, Ma Rainey's "Blue, Oh Blues," which is the same tune but with more elemental and bluesy lyrics that still use the repeated first line

> Blues, oh blues, oh blues
> Oh blues, oh blues, blues, oh blues
> I'm so blue, so blue I don't know what to do
> Oh blues, oh blues, oh blues

Jackson, who is identified as an African American but whose style and repertoire was much closer to white singers of the time, accompanies herself on guitar and treats the song as the folk ballad it apparently originally was. Other tunes she recorded are very much in the hillbilly style made famous by the Carter Family and Jimmy Rodgers.

For her part, Bessie Smith takes the stilted phrasing of the song and imparts a passionate and even sensual flavor that suggests the protagonist is not so much lamenting the loss of a lover as of losing the careless love that found him in the first place. Her exceptional breath control is on display in this song to the point where she occasionally crowds out the two horn players (cornetist Louis Armstrong and trombonist Charlie Green) with her. Although Green's contribution is not at the level of Smith's singing, Armstrong's blues-drenched phrases linking the vocal phrases further the emotional projection of the performance. When Smith enters on the last chorus (of the first take), her stentorian "Love, oh love, oh careless love" gives way to a snarling answer "Night and day, I weep and moan" before a wailing "You brought the wrong man into this life of mine / For my sins till judgment I'll atone" brings the song to a vivid conclusion.

MAMA'S GOT THE BLUES

Bessie Smith's recording of "Mama's Got the Blues" (Columbia A3900, April 28, 1923) might be a version of a song she was remembered singing on the stage as early as 1913 (Albertson 2003, 14). Entertainer Leigh Whipper recalled hearing her sing a song called "The Weary Blues" at the 81 in Atlanta around that time. Artie Matthews's "Weary Blues" became a jazz standard but was not published until 1915 and was not known as a vocal tune, so Whipper was probably referring to a different number.

"Mama's Got the Blues" begins with the lyric

> Some people say that the weary blues ain't bad
> Some people say the weary blues ain't bad
> But it's the worst old feeling that I've ever had

which may suggest the earlier tune, even if they were not identical. In any event, this blues was probably similar to any number of such songs for which Smith became known in her early days, possibly in imitation of Ma Rainey, who had been featuring blues since at least 1902. Another verse would have had resonance for an African American audience:

> Brown skin's deceitful, but a yellow man is worse
> Brown skin's deceitful, but a yellow man is worse
> I'm gonna get myself a black man and play safety first

However, the reference would probably have been lost on white audiences. Credited to singer Sarah Martin (who was ten years older than Smith and presumably had been touring with tent shows by the turn of the century), the song is basically a collection of stock blues images that show up on any number of blues recordings during the 1920s and that were probably part of the common stock of blues expression from at least the previous decade.

3

'TAIN'T NOBODY'S BIZ-NESS IF I DO

By 1921, Bessie Smith was a headliner on the black vaudeville and tent show circuits. Although she had apparently fronted only one show (*Liberty Belle* in Atlanta in 1921, in which she did an act as a male impersonator as well as her usual singing and dancing), she had become known as a featured attraction in other shows, with almost a decade of experience singing, dancing, and acting behind her along with stage partnerships with Wayne Burton and, in 1918, with Hazel Green. After a significant time using Atlanta as her home base, she relocated to Philadelphia in 1921, using Horan's Madhouse as a base of operations but making frequent appearances in Atlantic City (where she performed with Charlie Johnson's band at the Paradise Gardens during the 1922 summer season) and soon making occasional trips to New York City, where she began appearing in Harlem shows and in the recording studios.

At the end of January 1923, Smith was hired to play in Donald Heywood's revue *How Come*, which also featured New Orleans clarinetist Sidney Bechet in several scenes. Bechet later remembered that Smith participated in the show in Philadelphia (where it was resident at the Dunbar Theatre for a month) and possibly did some prior dates with it in Washington, DC (Chilton 1987, 56). Smith left the show after a month, apparently after a lively affair with Bechet and a contretemps with the star, Eddie Hunter.

Smith's romantic life was always vigorous, with frequent liaisons with both men and women marking the various stages of her career. At some point during the late 1910s she married a man named Earl Love, about whom nothing is known; he apparently died soon after the marriage, possibly during World War I. Following her affair with Bechet, Smith was introduced to Jack Gee, who worked as a security guard. Legend has it that on their first date Gee was involved in an altercation and was either shot or stabbed, earning him a five-week stay in the hospital. During this time Smith stayed with him, and her concern blossomed into love, leading to their marriage in June of 1923. This relationship caused much turbulence in Smith's life, with Gee attempting to take over her career and establish himself in show business, but he succeeded only in alienating his wife and having a long-term affair with Gertrude Saunders, one of her competitors. Frequent physical altercations, splits, and reunions marked their union, which effectively (if not legally) ended in 1929, after Gee essentially kidnapped their adopted son, Jack Gee Jr.

One element of stability (if not peace) in Smith's life in Philadelphia was the presence of her family, including her sister Viola (who had raised the Smith siblings after the death of their parents) and sister-in-law Maude (who was married to her brother Clarence, who also toured extensively on the Theatre Owner's Booking Agents [TOBA] circuit). Smith brought them there in 1926 to get them out of the South as well as to provide some support for herself. It was to Philadelphia that she returned between tours to spend time with her family and visit her stepson, who was raised for the most part by Viola. Ultimately, she was brought back there after her death and interred in Mount Lawn Cemetery.

One benefit of being based in Philadelphia was the relatively easy access to New York City, where Smith was to do much work during the 1920s. Of more importance to her legacy was the proximity of numerous recording studios in the area.

RACE RECORDS

African American musicians and entertainers had been making records since the beginning of the industry. One of the first successful recording artists was George W. Johnson, who made extremely popular cylinder recordings of "The Whistling Coon" and "The Laughing Song" for Victor in the early 1890s. Numerous gospel and popular black vocal quartets were also recording during this period, as were Broadway and vaudeville stars George Walker and Bert Williams. It was Williams who became the first great crossover act. His significant popularity in all-black shows in the early decades of the twentieth century gave way to featured performances in the otherwise all-white Ziegfeld Follies of 1910 and almost every following season until 1919, during which period he also made many popular recordings for Columbia. Several black string bands and concert artists (tenor Roland Hayes, pianist Revella Hughes, and violinist Kemper Harreld) recorded before the beginning of Classic Blues era as did several syncopated dance bands (heavily influenced by ragtime and circus bands), such as those led by W. C. Handy and James Reese Europe. Europe's famous 369th Hellfighters military band recorded extensively on its return from World War I before he was murdered by one of his own musicians.

Although some of these recordings were commercially successful, none of them was produced specifically for black audiences until after 1920. It was not until Mamie Smith's success (see chapter 1) that recording companies came to realize the largely untapped potential of the African American consumer. As has been discussed, Smith began recording for the OKeh company in February 1920, producing two fairly ordinary pop tunes that sold well enough to bring her back in August, at which time she recorded "Crazy Blues." The incredible (and virtually instant) success of that record caused OKeh's producer Ralph Peer and recording director Fred Hager to begin a program of recruiting African American musicians and singers to record popular, mainly blues and jazz-based numbers as part of their regular catalog.

Beginning in 1918, OKeh had produced a long and varied record output touching every conceivable stylistic base other than African American music. One early staple was white vaudeville performers such as Collins and Harlan, Arthur Fields, Billy Murray, and Ada Jones, who featured minstrel and blackface songs in their stage shows. The company began recording jazz bands as early as November 1918 with the Original New Orleans Jazz Band (featuring the New Orleans Creole clarinetist Achille Baquet, who passed for white) and the Louisiana Five in May of the following year, although most of what was credited as "jazz" on the label were basically white dance bands of ten or more pieces, occasionally enlivened by a short "hot" solo that rarely strayed far from the melody. It was Mamie Smith's emergence that showed

Peer how marketable African American music (at least the popular music heard onstage) could be. By early 1921 OKeh was releasing an increasing number of records by singers such as Smith and Eva Taylor on their 4500 series, which seems to have been reserved primarily for jazz and jazz-influenced dance music (by both white and black bands). By the middle of 1921, OKeh introduced its 8000 series, which was initially dominated by African American women including Virginia Liston, Sarah Martin, Sippie Wallace, and later Taylor and Smith singing some version of blues. By 1923, black jazz bands such as those led by Clarence Williams, Bennie Moten, King Oliver, and Fess Williams were regular contributors to the series, but artistically and financially the most lucrative relationship began in November 1925 when Louis Armstrong was signed. Peer was named the recording director of this catalog, which he referred to as "race records," a designation that came to be used by the industry for recordings aimed at specific (especially African American) markets. He was inspired to seek out and hire new singers and bands, even to the extent of taking portable recording equipment on field trips outside the New York and Chicago studios to record regional talent in Atlanta, New Orleans, and St. Louis, among other locations.

The success of the OKeh 8000 series encouraged other companies to develop similar marketing strategies targeting African American audiences. Some smaller companies such as Paramount, Gennett, Vocalion, and Emerson focused primarily on the new dance styles featuring black musicians, while two—Black Patti and Black Swan—dealt exclusively with African American artists, making a specific race designation unnecessary. For Columbia, which had vied with Victor as the premier recording company during the first two decades of the twentieth century, its successful series of recordings of blues singers and the sudden success of Bessie Smith's first records compelled them to begin a specific race series. The 13000 series was inaugurated in the fall of 1923 by Smith, whose record "Whoa Tillie, Take Your Time"/"My Sweetie Went Away" (October 15, 1923, Col 13000) was the first issue. "Far Away Blues"/"I'm Going Back to My Used to Be" was recorded ten days before (October 5, 1923, Col 13007) and "Sam Jones Blues"/"St. Louis Gal" (September 26, 1923, Col 13005) three weeks earlier but were released later. The fact that the first coupling on the race series was not a blues or even a tune by a black songwriter suggests that Columbia put more weight on the artist than the repertoire in designating audience direction. Within two months the series was renumbered in the 14000 sequence and again began with a Bessie Smith issue ("Chicago Bound Blues"/"Mistreatin' Daddy" December 4, 1923, Col 14000), which was much more authentic in terms of blues expression. This series continued until the early 1930s, with the overwhelming focus on blues singers with occasional jazz bands included (although most of these featured singers). Victor did not establish its separate race catalog until the end of the 1920s, by which time the Depression had severely contracted the industry.

The material on these race records consisted of a loose grouping of musical acts assumed to appeal to black audiences. Occasionally white groups inclined to a more jazzy or bluesy style would be included in race catalogs, and African American performers thought to have crossover appeal would be included in the main catalog. Trade magazines published separate lists of top recordings for the mainstream and "race" categories, although by 1949, the change in musical tastes and gradual rejection of the term "race" (which had been a positive affirmation in the 1910s and 1920s) facilitated the change in category to "rhythm and blues."

RECORDING AUDITIONS

Bessie Smith apparently made several audition records before her first issued disc for Columbia in February 1923. A persistent legend is that she did a test record for Harry Pace's Black Swan company in 1921, possibly following her relocation to Philadelphia. Whether or not the music was acceptable, the rather refined Pace was apparently horrified by Smith's down-home dress and bearing (she reportedly interrupted a take to spit on the floor and made no attempt to restrain her manners or language) and refused to sign her. It is interesting to speculate how the fortunes of both the singer and the company might have been different had Pace overlooked what he obviously considered a poor reflection on his perception of race. Had Pace's former partner, W. C. Handy (an admirer of the singer, as will be seen) still been part of the company, Smith might have been hired and Black Swan might have successfully negotiated the pitfalls that bankrupted it in 1923, just as Smith's recording career was beginning.

An interesting advertisement in the *Chicago Defender* newspaper on February 12, 1921, mentions that Smith had just recorded for Emerson and that the records would be out in March. No mention of these by any musicians nor any trace of them has been found, so it could well be that it was a publicity gimmick or possibly an idea that was never carried through to fruition. In another similar ad from May 21 of that year in the *Philadelphia Tribune*, Smith was credited with having "Hits on Columbia Records," which was not to happen for two years. Another legend was that she auditioned for Thomas Edison who also refused to sign her.

In January 1923, Smith made a test recording accompanied by clarinetist Sidney Bechet (with whom she was appearing in the show *How Come*). Bechet claimed in his autobiography that he was the driving force behind this session, which was done for OKeh (Bechet 1982, 186), although Clarence Williams claimed that he was part of the band and that it was for Columbia (Shapiro and Hentoff 1955, 241). In some ways, Williams's version makes more sense, especially given that Bechet was renowned for his ability to spin a story. Williams was the pianist on Smith's first issued sides from February 16 of that year, and the two of them had also made several rejected takes the day before. Perhaps the session from the previous month had been more of an audition—the song recorded was (according to both Bechet and Williams) "I Wish I Could Shimmy Like My Sister Kate," a song known from Bechet's younger days in New Orleans and one for which Williams claimed authorship. Standard discographies cite a jazz band including Bubber Miley on cornet, Charlie Irvis on trombone, and Buddy Christian on banjo, largely (one would imagine) on the strength that these were musicians who recorded with Williams frequently at the time (Bechet also played with Miley and Irvis during his short stint with Duke Ellington's band during the summer of 1924, which might also influence the story a bit).

The story of how Bessie Smith was finally signed by Columbia to make her first recordings is one with several variants. The main producer of popular music at Columbia during the 1920s was Frank Walker, who also did a great deal to record country music during that period and later as well. His counterpart at OKeh was Ralph Peer, who had a similarly open mind to recording black music (a liberal attitude not shared by Victor's recording director Eddie King). Walker had apparently heard Smith sing several years before and remembered her compelling voice and way of performing. According to a later interview, he dispatched Clarence Williams, who had been recording for Columbia for several months and who was in any case well known as a music publisher and promoter, to go "down south" to find Bessie Smith. Williams did find her, but according to an interview with him, he had to go no farther than Washington, DC, where he knew she was performing (Shapiro and Hentoff 1955, 239–41). Walker remembered her as "tall and fat and scared to death," although those nerves seem not to have influenced her performance. Though the first session (or first two sessions, if you count the one with Bechet) were rejected—possibly due to poor performance or technical issues common at the time—the third session produced one of Smith's best and most successful records.

DOWNHEARTED BLUES

As discussed in chapter 1, "Downhearted Blues" was a composition by Alberta Hunter and Lovie Austin that represented one of the most popular and significant songs of the Classic Blues era. Published in 1922, Hunter's own recording was extremely successful and influential, as were her live performances with King Oliver's band at the Dreamland Cafe in Chicago during that period. In fact, Hunter, one of the few popular entertainers of the day with good business sense, proposed to Frank Walker in a letter that he assign the tune to a singer at Columbia and that he also hire Oliver's band (Albertson 2003, 33). Walker's counterproposal—that she record the tune with Oliver for Columbia—was not feasible due to her contract with Paramount, although he did take part of the suggestion and had Bessie Smith record it as her first release, showing the regard he must have had for her talents and marketing potential.

The most compelling question facing anyone attempting to address what made Bessie Smith the singer she was is what set her apart from her contemporaries. From the first notes of her first release her vocal quality and delivery put the world on notice that something very new was happening. Although it clearly wasn't new to the southern black audiences for which she had performed for the previous fifteen years or so, it was a vastly different product than the general record-buying public was accustomed to.

Peter Muir, in a survey of blues compositions and recordings prior to the Classic Blues era (Muir 2010, 88), has cited two distinct strains of blues taxonomy: homeopathic (dealing with one's blue feelings by lamenting those feelings in song) and allopathic (an alternate way of dealing with hardship or depression emphasizing happy, escapist song). This separation is useful when trying to explain the change from the style of the cabaret singers like Mamie Smith and even Alberta Hunter to the "down-home" styles of Bessie Smith and Ma Rainey. The versions of "Downhearted Blues" by Hunter and Smith use essentially the same lyrics and were recorded only seven months apart but convey vastly different moods. The Hunter recording (discussed in chapter 1) has a triumphant sound—the snappy arrangement with military horns highlights the singer's shouting declaration of lost love, which gives the impression of defiance more than resignation, especially the final verse (which occurs as the second verse in the sheet music):

> Got the world in a jug, the stopper's in my hand
> Got the world in a jug (lawd), got the stopper in my hand
> If you want me sweet papa, you gotta come under my command

While Hunter's version could be classed as allopathic to a degree, Bessie Smith channels the more southern, folk element that emphasizes a homeopathic musical remedy for the blues. Using virtually the same lyrics (Smith omits Hunter's first chorus: "He mistreated me . . ." due, one would imagine, to the fact that her version is slower and something had to be cut), Smith conveys a dark, sorrowful quality to the performance that emphasizes the loss rather than the triumph. By lowering the key from the published E flat to C major, Smith darkens the performance, to which the heaviness of her voice, the sparseness of the accompaniment, and her way of sustaining notes—not merely holding them, but coloring them with moans, slides, bends, and blue notes—contributes to the transformation. Even Clarence Williams's fairly inept accompaniment (he gets lost in the second "I ain't never loved . . ." chorus, but she manages to bring him back) cannot demolish the mood. She ends the performance as Hunter did, with the defiant "Got the world in a jug" verse, but in her hands it sounds a note of irony rather than optimism.

The success of Smith's recording of "Downhearted Blues" (Columbia A-3844, February 16, 1923) spawned numerous competing versions. Clarence Williams accompanied his wife Eva Taylor on the tune for OKeh one month before he was in the studio with Smith, while at about the same time singer Monette Moore recorded the tune for Pathe in a version that compares favorably with Smith's. Fletcher Henderson accompanied Mary Straine in a screechy version for Black Swan in April and then was with Mary Gover for Pathe in June on a version that is virtually a copy of Smith's, even down to the sequence of verses (which vary in the other performances). Recordings by Lillian Harris (for Banner) and Lucille Hegamin (Cameo) were also made that spring, followed by Hazel Meyers (Bell) in December, finishing the initial vogue for the song.

The only one of the abovementioned recordings slower than Smith's was the one by Hazel Meyers. Even with the more lugubrious tempo, Meyers's mannered singing and precise articulation does not create the mournful quality of Smith's record, which outsold all competitors (including the one by the composer).

From the first notes of this performance, Bessie Smith comes across as confident in her abilities and assured in her technique. Several accounts have suggested how nervous and tentative she was before she succeeded on the released take, but with more than ten years of professional stage performance and several recording auditions behind her, Smith began her recording career with extensive experience.

'TAIN'T NOBODY'S BIZ-NESS IF I DO

On this, the last recording session before Smith's new contract took effect (symbolized by Fletcher Henderson replacing Clarence Williams as accompanist), two tunes were recorded that had been attempted before. "Keeps on a-Rainin'" had been recorded at the session that produced "Downhearted Blues" and again on a session from early March but was rejected both times. "'Tain't Nobody's Biz-ness" was likewise rejected from the March session as well as from her first aborted recording date with Williams. The third time was apparently the charm for each, although neither is an unqualified success.

"'Tain't Nobody's Biz-ness" (Columbia A-3898, April 26, 1923) was a vaudeville song by pianists Everett Robbins and Porter Grainger, both of whom worked as accompanists for Mamie Smith during the 1920s. Grainger later accompanied Bessie Smith and directed her in the revue *Mississippi Days* in 1928 as well as appearing on a number of recordings from that period. The song itself is unremarkable. After a sixteen-bar verse setting the scene:

> There ain't nothing I can do or nothing I can say
> That folks don't criticize me
> But I'm goin' to do just as I want to anyway
> And don't care if they all despise me

the song goes into a series of eight-measure verses (which can be heard as a repeating period, creating a sixteen-measure form) in which the final four measures are always a repeat of the song title. The series of patter-like first sections are obviously geared to performance onstage. The lyrics are interesting only for the autobiographical content in Smith's performance; for example, "If I should take a notion to jump into the ocean—'Tain't nobody's biz-ness if I do" or the final verse:

> I'd rather my man would hit me
> Than to jump up right and quit me
> 'Tain't nobody's bizness if I do (do, do, do)
> I swear I won't call no copper
> If I'm beat up by my poppa 'Tain't nobody's bizness if I do (if I do)

The defiant lyrics and mood of this song (to say nothing of the easy reference to domestic violence) make it easy to assume that it was composed specifically for Bessie Smith, which was not the case. By the time her recording was released, it had already been recorded at least six times by various singers. The song went on to have a long and successful life, being revived numerous times over the next decades, most notably by blues singer Jimmy Witherspoon in 1950.

Smith's initial contract with Columbia called for her to make recordings for $125 per issued side—a not inconsiderable fee in those days. The issue was that she did not in fact sign with Columbia, but with Clarence Williams, who was apparently acting as an agent (unbeknownst to either Smith or Columbia). In addition to taking half the fee, he also made sure that he played on the recording session and that she recorded several of his compositions and publications, netting him considerable royalties. When Smith became involved with Jack Gee, Gee apparently began overseeing some of her business affairs and quickly discovered Williams's machinations. There followed a legendary scene of confrontation and apparent violence that ended with Williams under his desk and Smith free of her obligation to him (Albertson 2003, 36). This is a good story, but according to Albertson, the severance occurred after six records were made—the discographies list two more after that and in any event Williams returned to play on Smith sessions later in the decade.

What is certain is that Smith signed a contract with Frank Walker and Columbia on April 20, 1923, for a one-year period during which she would be paid $125 per record for twelve issued recordings. Albertson and other commentators have interpreted this to be $125 per side, but based on the consistent release schedule, I believe it was per record (each of which had two sides). This $1,500 income equaled the average annual income of a full-time worker during 1923 and presumably exceeded that which most African American laborers took home. Columbia also profited from this association—Smith's recording of "Downhearted Blues" may have sold as many as two million copies during the 1920s (with perhaps 750,000 being sold during its first month of release).

As mentioned, these were the last two titles recorded and released before Smith started fulfilling her new contract with Columbia, which was signed on April 20, 1923, making it curious that she was still recording with Clarence Williams after that date. Presumably he was still smarting from the confrontation with Smith and Gee—perhaps these last two sides were to complete the contract he had with Columbia or the dates are simply wrong. Edward Brooks suggests "'Tain't Nobody's Biz-ness" was recorded on April 11, although he cites April 26 for "Keeps on a-Rainin'." The matrix numbers for both records suggest a date closer to the earlier one, although they were sometimes altered by the company for ease of process.

MY SWEETIE WENT AWAY

The first of Bessie Smith's recordings to be released in Columbia's race record series was "My Sweetie Went Away" (Columbia 13000, October 15, 1923), a show tune composed by the white composers Roy Turk and Lou Handman with no evident African American influences in musical language beyond the standard theme of loss. As with most popular tunes of this period, "My Sweetie" consists of a verse setting up the action and a chorus functioning as the refrain. In this case both sections are in AABA form, with the verse being sixteen bars and the chorus twice as long. The harmonic patterns of each section are considerably more involved and chromatic than most tunes of the era, which may have been the reason it was infrequently recorded—during the 1920s it was recorded eight times in America (four times more in South America and Europe), with Fletcher Henderson's band version being the only other recording of the song by an African American.

The two verses tell the story of Lou, who in the first verse comes home to find that Sue, his sweetie, has left—"without a word, his turtle-dove had flown"—and in the second verse is in the process of committing suicide. The chorus is a lament he sings about how she left "but she didn't say where, she didn't say when, she didn't say why, or bid me good-bye," following which he says he's "got the blues" because "my triflin' mamma left her papa all alone"—a quote common to blues tunes of the period. Aside from this tangential language, any blues inflection is absent from the sheet music.

Smith turns the rather ordinary lyrics into a bluesy torch song: her sliding between notes—for example, on "try-in' [to forget]" in the chorus B section—transforms an ordinary and fairly square melodic cell into something characteristic and far more emotionally charged. At the end of the same section she holds a note (on "lone") while the clarinet plays a break. When she comes back in, the printed lyrics are "I groan, my sweetie went away" but rather than connect the first two syllables to the following phrase, she uses them as an answer to her own held note and effectively completes the clarinet player's musical idea as well. In addition to these stylistic inflections, Smith reverses the gender of the pronouns, so instead of Lou being the wronged party, she sings about Sue's loss, possibly making the lyrics self-reflexive and investing a degree of realism in the performance that would not have been there had she sung the original version.

Why Columbia picked this number to be the first of its race record series might seem somewhat mysterious until it becomes clear that they were marketing the singer rather than the song in this case. Clearly, Frank Walker felt that Bessie Smith's approach, style, and appeal were specifically African American and thus designed to appeal to black consumers. The other side made that day was "Whoa, Tillie, Take Your Time" by the black songwriting team of Henry Creamer and Turner Layton, although this song has, if anything, fewer overt African American cultural signifiers. The group accompanying her on the previous unreleased session on which "My Sweetie" was recorded was credited as "Her Down Home Trio," although to be fair, that designation was used on the session from April 11, 1923, which produced two tunes ("Aggravatin' Papa" and "Beale Street Mama") also by Roy Turk, this time with the white pianist and composer J. Russel Robinson. The group on the October session was listed as simply "clarinet and piano," which are reputed to be pianist Jimmy Jones, who was known to have toured with the singer around this time, and clarinetist George Baquet. Baquet was a legendary New Orleans clarinetist whose family had been central to the music scene in that city since the beginning of the century. He had studied with Lorenzo Tio Jr. and left to tour with the Original Creole Band, perhaps the first black jazz band to appear on the Pantages (white) vaudeville circuit. He subsequently settled in Philadelphia, playing in the pit band of the Lafayette Theatre, where he presumably became acquainted with Smith. Baquet recorded infrequently (other than this session, he can be heard on several at the end of the decade with Jelly Roll Morton and a live recording in Philadelphia shortly before he died in 1949), but the tone, phrasing, and execution on this date (particularly his solo on "Whoa, Tillie") seem more like him than the other contender, Ernest Elliot, who accompanied numerous blues singers in the 1920s.

THE FIRST YEAR

During the first year of her recording career with Columbia (February 1923–January 1924), Bessie Smith recorded forty-six titles, of which thirty-two were released. From April 28, 1923, until the beginning of April 1924, twelve (double-sided) records were released, fulfilling her contract, which must not have included the two sides recorded on April 26. Presumably, the contretemps between Clarence Williams and Smith and Jack Gee took place at that time—Fletcher Henderson replaces Williams on April 28 and appears on about half the released sides from this period (Williams begins to reappear in late 1925 and occasionally thereafter).

For the most part, the recordings made during that first calendar year period are obvious market testing. Frank Walker was the likely party who had the final say on the repertoire, which he divided evenly between blues and popular songs. Walker was also responsible for a certain amount of Smith's professional management, booking tours and personal appearances, although he is not known to have ever toured with her. He also erred on the side of musical conservatism by using a solo piano accompaniment on most of the issued recordings, the exceptions being three sessions on which a clarinet is added, one session with a clarinet and banjo, one tune using a second piano, two adding a guitar, and one with another singer. Even on the recordings with the clarinet, the extra vocalized instrument does not participate in any significant call-and-response with the singer. On both "Beale Street Mama (Papa)" and "Aggravatin' Papa," the clarinet and banjo play the introduction and the second chorus, remaining mum during Smith's verse and chorus and joining her only on the final section. Baquet's playing on "Whoa Tillie" and "My Sweetie" have been discussed, and Don Redman's clarinet playing on "Chicago Bound Blues" and "Mistreatin' Daddy" is somewhat more integrated into the performance, although his fills at the end of the vocal phrases on the former are still detached from the emotional impetus of Smith's performance and largely free of any blues feeling. On "Eavesdropper's Blues" his playing is again repetitious, showing little or no stylistic engagement, while "Haunted House Blues" utilizes a novelty approach, including some heavy-handed humor in many of his responses.

Two interesting tracks featuring a duet between Smith and her chief competitor on Columbia's race series, Clara Smith, ultimately fail due to the essential dullness of the material and the restrictive nature of the arrangement, which allows for no real give and take between the singers. Far more successful is their one follow-up collaboration "My Man

Blues" from September 1, 1925 (Columbia 14098-D), which might re-create some of the stage chemistry between Bessie Smith and her World War I–era partner Hazel Green. Here, the two Smiths trade four-measure phrases (the unusual song structure is a twelve-bar blues with the middle four measures omitted) discussing their man, Charlie Gray. As they go back and forth, there is at least the impression of spontaneity between the singers, with the two joining in a loose harmony at the end as they recognize that they will have to share their man "on cooperation plan / ain't nothing different, 'cause he's our two-time man."

For the last session of the contract period (spread out over three days on January 8, 9, and 10, 1924), several approaches were tried in terms of accompaniment. As mentioned, Don Redman was added on clarinet on "Eavesdropper's Blues" and "Haunted House Blues" and a guitar (Harry Reser) was added to "Frosty Mornin' Blues" and "Easy Come, Easy Go Blues" (two unreleased and lost tracks from January 10 have the tantalizing credit "Bessie Smith accompanied by her Jazz Band"). Though Redman's clarinet was not impressive—he was the chief arranger and leader of the saxophone section in Fletcher Henderson's dance band at the time and presumably added at Henderson's behest—Reser's guitar provided an interesting timbre that called to mind the more rural southern tradition. This is remarkable considering that Reser was a white musician who was known principally as a banjo virtuoso rather than a jazz or blues player. His accompaniment is very much to the fore on these recordings, with Jimmy Jones's piano audible but strictly in the background. The lighter, more intimate sound of the guitar inspires a more intimate vocal quality by Smith—not, as her biographer Chris Albertson surmises, a reflection of her fatigue from continual performing (Albertson 2003, 63). Apparently, the sound suggested by the guitar generated enough positive record sales and enthusiasm by Walker and probably Smith to warrant repeating.

FOLK INFLUENCE

A March 22, 1924, clipping from the *Pittsburgh Defender* announced that Bessie Smith would be doing a broadcast on WCAE the following Friday night, accompanied by pianist Irving Johns and violinist John

Snow. Johns was her regular accompanist at this time, although it is not clear if Snow was a regular part of her stage show. Whether he was a regular or just added for the broadcast, it is interesting that someone (either Smith, Frank Walker, or someone else) decided that a violin was a suitable accompaniment for her blues. Violins were used in dance music of the period primarily to play melody; the day of the jazz violin was still a few years off, although Joe Venuti, Stuff Smith, and Eddie South were all making records during the 1920s. In New Orleans, for example, violinists were often the members of the band with the most technical training, so it would fall to them to learn new music, teach it to the other less accomplished musicians, and direct the group onstage. In the minds of most consumers, the solo violin was an instrument that suggested country (or hillbilly) music when not used in the classical realm.

Given the fact that Smith had just finished a tour (highlighted by an extended residency at the Lincoln and the Star Theaters in Pittsburgh during the first part of the year), it is a reasonable assumption that the tunes she recorded over five days in April to begin her next Columbia contract were things she had been featuring in her act, especially considering the participation of Johns and the inclusion of the violin. This suspicion is furthered by the fact that three of the eight released tunes from these sessions were composed by Smith and Johns (up to this point, only one song recorded by Smith—"Jailhouse Blues"—was her own composition), with two others being covers of tunes by Ma Rainey.

The sudden change in direction for Bessie Smith's recording career may have been a product of one or more events: her increased popularity due to her first year's recordings and extended touring allowing her more input into her recorded repertoire, a perception that she was more suited to vernacular blues performances as opposed to standard popular fare, or possibly market research suggesting that her appeal was to a more rural, southern audience that would better respond to folk-based material. A combination of these three possibilities would seem to be the most likely, with the third being perhaps the most determining factor. The idea that market research (whatever that might have meant to 1924 record companies) may have inspired the changes in repertoire and accompaniment on her April sessions is supported by the fact that a similar approach seems to have been taken with Clara Smith, who appears to have had a similar contract with Columbia.

Between her first session in May 1923 through the end of January 1924, Clara Smith released twelve records, as did Bessie Smith during the same period. On her last sessions in January, she too was accompanied by several very different groups, from a jazz band made up of musicians from Henderson's band to a folky trio of mandolin or harmonica, guitar, and kazoo, suggesting some experimental thought on the part of Frank Walker. The two tunes she made accompanied by the jazz band were fast, sophisticated, and completely unlike anything Bessie Smith ever recorded (although the two rejected takes previously mentioned are a tantalizing glimpse of yet another direction in which she might have gone). Both Clara and Bessie Smith resumed recording in April when presumably their contracts were renewed and each recorded a series of titles more heavily geared to the rural southern sound than had been in their repertoire previously. During the three weeks between April 10 and the end of the month, Clara Smith had seven released tunes: the first two accompanied by just Henderson and Don Redman and the others featuring a combination of guitars and ukuleles in support of more traditional blues and folk material.

Bessie Smith's recordings from April 4 through 9 likewise feature a variety of accompaniments from violin and guitar, to violin and piano, to just piano, with a single session taking place on April 23 producing two rejected sides on which she was accompanied by piano, banjo, and ukulele (Clara Smith recorded the same day with the same musicians, releasing one of two tunes). On Bessie Smith's recordings, her regular pianist Irving (or Irvin) Johns is featured instrumentally as well as being given co-composer credit with the singer on "Sorrowful Blues," "Pinchbacks, Take 'Em Away," and "Rocking Chair Blues." This inclusion of Johns, who accompanied her on her winter theater tour leading up to these sessions, may also signal that the tunes recorded were things they had already been performing, not necessarily the case over the course of the previous year.

SORROWFUL BLUES

This piece (Columbia 14020-D, April 4, 1924) was only the second tune Smith recorded for which she was given composer credit. After an introduction featuring four bars of scat singing, the tune itself evolves through four choruses of blues that seem to have little or no thematic relation. David Evans has suggested that indeed the choruses were interrelated and that Smith (and Johns) were trying to establish a symmetrical structure (Evans 1982, 69). This argument seems far-fetched, especially given the casual way in which Bessie Smith was known to treat her own recordings and her professional life in general. Each of the verses seems to come from a common stock of southern folk expression. For example, the third chorus

> I got nineteen men and I want one more
> I got nineteen men and I want one more
> If I get that one man, I'll let that other nineteen go

can also be heard on Ida Cox's "Chicago Monkey Man Blues" (on which Cox has only fourteen men), and Charlie Manson's "Nineteen Woman Blues," among others. The third verse

> I'm gonna tell you daddy like the Chinaman told the Jew
> I'm gonna tell you daddy like the Chinaman told the Jew
> If you don't likee me, me sure don't likee you

represents some interesting elements of racism that appear extraordinary to today's sensibilities and recall the words to "Crazy Blues" quoted in chapter 1.

Smith's version of this tune produces a sound completely unlike any of her previous or subsequent recordings. Accompanied by only violinist Robert Robbins and guitarist John Griffin, Smith frees up her phrasing and sings in a more intimate style that for the first time in her discography also allows for some instrumental interplay at the end of the vocal phrases. Nothing is known about either Robbins or Griffin, but the violinist is clearly at home with the style of Country Blues. It would be interesting to know whether he was a white or black player and what musical tradition he came from, although he is obviously comfortable improvising discrete backgrounds to the vocal and also foreground responses answering her vocal lines. Here, Smith adopts a "mean" sound, especially at the beginning of the record, calling to mind Ma Rainey and possibly earlier and more traditional black singers in the South. She also leaves more room at the end of her phrases for Robbins to craft his own answers using slides, double-stops, and trills that connect with Smith's emotional intensity in a way that, for example, Redman's clarinet did not.

PINCHBACKS, TAKE 'EM AWAY

This tune (Columbia 14025-D, April 4, 1924), again credited to Smith and Johns, is unusual in several regards. First, it is the fastest tempo attempted by the singer so far in her recording career (and among the fastest she ever recorded), although there are clearly some differences of opinion between the two performers regarding the correct speed. Second, as Edward Brooks points out, "Pinchbacks" is clearly derived from the popular 1912 British song "It's a Long Way to Tipperary" by Jack Judge and Harry Williams, which became a popular World War I standard (Brooks 1982, 46). Finally, it is the best example we have of how Bessie Smith probably sounded on a theater stage.

Whether or not she had actually performed this song on her recent tour, she had played several theaters and at least one broadcast during the three months or so before this session with Johns as her principal and perhaps only accompanist, so it is reasonable to assume that the interaction they produce here is a reflection of what they had onstage. This recording was made at the end of Smith's first really successful tour, establishing her as a national act on the heels of her successful recordings. Johns had been her music director and main accompanist since at least June 1923, and the two of them had been on a tour of major TOBA theaters through the Midwest, Gulf Coast, and southeastern United States, breaking attendance records in numerous places and even playing occasionally for white audiences. It appeared that the days of appearing in fly-by-night tent shows and with minstrel companies were a thing of the past for Bessie Smith.

Part of the disagreement about the tempo on "Pinchbacks" can be blamed on the fact that the song is really written in half time—the beat of this tune is equivalent to the eighth note of "Tipperary," creating the disagreement about the pulse. During the introduction, Johns's accompaniment sets a rollicking mood that suggests boogie-woogie, although it never quite settles into the familiar eight-to-the-bar pattern that was even then a commonly heard flavor in the work of black pianists working in the blues tradition. After the piano introduction, Smith enters with a bit of stagecraft: she establishes the mood of the song over a piano vamp, stating that she is addressing the women in the audience in order to warn them about the "sweet men" who were up to no good. The verse then identifies her "sweet man" as one who refused to work and lived off her earnings. The first chorus laments that the man is an albatross around her neck and she further instructs her audience to

Get a working man when you marry and let all these sweet men be
Now it takes money to run a business and with me I know you girls will agree.

By the second chorus, the lyrics are changed to define the title of the song, changing "sweet men" to "pinchbacks," which may derive from a term that meant a fake or an imitation (presumably of a good husband, in this context).

Johns's playing on this track is quite flashy by comparison with Smith's previous piano accompanists, who were not regarded as particularly skilled musicians (Clarence Williams) or sympathetic blues players (Fletcher Henderson). His previous appearances on record with Bessie Smith occurred in September 1923 and may have been the warmup to the fall/winter tour. On "Jaihouse Blues," he also hints at boogie-woogie (albeit at a slow tempo) and improves the tune, adding a chromatic chord on the sixth measure that is not in Clarence Williams's published version. This song is the first and, until the April 1924 sessions, only song recorded by Smith on which she is given composer credit (with Williams). The other two recordings on which Johns accompanies Smith ("St. Louis Gal" on which there is a second piano as well and "Sam Jones Blues") are less interesting and tend more toward novelty or pop songs. His accompaniment on "Pinchbacks" is highly energetic and quite florid at times, although he doesn't come off well in his solo break during the first chorus. By the second chorus he has established a proto-boogie bass line that drives the singer into some highly charged shouting that would have brought an audience to its feet in live performance.

It is tempting to read some autobiographical content into Smith's lyrics to "Pinchbacks." Her marital situation with Jack Gee devolved into a cycle of violence and systematic cheating and abuse on both sides, but in April 1924 they had just passed their first anniversary as a couple and things were apparently relatively placid. Gee was traveling with Smith and Johns and overseeing some of the details of the tour, including salary negotiation and collection, although his business acumen was questionable at best. Nevertheless, the way the situation was to develop over the next few years makes "Pinchbacks, Take 'Em Away" seem prescient.

4

I AIN'T GONNA PLAY NO SECOND FIDDLE

After the first series of recordings on her new contract were made and released, a decision was apparently made that Bessie Smith was better accompanied by more urban, sophisticated musicians playing in the current jazz style. Whether this was a decision made by her, by Frank Walker, or by them both is difficult to determine, although it is an incontrovertible truth that the business of recording Classic Blues singers changed at that point. Albertson points out that articles in the black press from this period began to sound the "death knell" of the style, which at that point was four years old dated from Mamie Smith's first success (Albertson 2003, 63). The introduction of more rural elements to the recordings of Bessie Smith and Clara Smith were, while musically interesting in retrospect, apparently not commercially viable, as the experiment was not repeated.

A look at the discographies of the most popular African American singers of the first three years of the 1920s shows a marked decline in issued recordings beginning in 1924. Of all the singers active in the wake of the success of "Crazy Blues," only Ethel Waters survived relatively well on disc through the decade. Mamie Smith, Lucille Hegamin, Trixie Smith, Sippie Wallace, and even Alberta Hunter saw a significant reduction in the frequency of their trips to the recording studios, and this might be attributed to consumer fatigue and the increased emphasis on jazz in popular music. Bessie Smith, Clara Smith, and Ma Rainey were all relative newcomers to the field by 1924 and had significant followings among southern black audiences and, in Bessie Smith's case, some white audiences as well (Eva Taylor had recorded a few things in 1922, but her recording career began more or less in 1923 and was driven by her husband, Clarence Williams, who kept her busy well into the 1930s). Other singers such as Rosa Henderson saw a brief pause but then a resumption later in the decade, although the material they recorded was more reflective of an earlier, more rural blues style.

Columbia's attempt to present their two Smiths in musically rural garb in the first half of 1924 should be seen as an informed but ultimately unsuccessful effort to capitalize on their perceived folk appeal. Though this logic makes sense, the target audience apparently wanted to hear a blending of these singers' styles with the cutting edge of black dance music in New York. A comparison of the recordings of both singers from the summer of 1924 through the end of the year shows a similar approach—clearly both were on the same type of contract and even recorded at similar times. Usually, Bessie Smith was first, using members of the Henderson band including Henderson himself, and then Clara Smith would do sessions a few days or a week later using similar musicians but with a different pianist, often Porter Grainger, who may have been her accompanist on tour at that time.

An interesting corollary to the Smith nexus is singer Maggie Jones, who recorded for Paramount under her real name, Fae Barnes, beginning in 1923. As Jones she recorded an initial session for Columbia in October 1924 with pianist Lemuel Fowler, which I believe was an audition session. The results apparently sold well enough, and it appears that Columbia put her under the same type of contract already mentioned, as she released twelve recordings (twenty-four sides) between November 1924 and the following September (she made a further six released sides in May and June 1926). Though not as commanding a singer as either of the Smiths, Jones did bring an air of authenticity to her blues performances and was recorded in numerous different settings featuring some of the musicians who were regularly in the Columbia studios at the time from the Henderson band (Fletcher Henderson, Louis Armstrong, Charlie Green, and Joe Smith) as well as musicians working with the banjo player/contractor Elmer Snowden (Bob Fuller, Louis Hooper, and Snowden himself). A single session accompanied by only "Alabama Joe"—a pseudonym for the white guitarist Roy Smeck—

was a nod to the rural blues with which Jones was presumably familiar from her youth in Texas.

On two sessions her versatility was on display, suggesting that Walker and Columbia may have been grooming her as the successor to the more down-home singers they had been featuring. One session, with members of the Henderson band, has been discussed in chapter 2. "Cheatin' on Me" and "Mama, Won't You Come and Ma-ma Me" from May 1925 were done as a test session for the new electrical recording process on the same day that Bessie Smith's "Cake Walking Babies" was recorded (using the same band). A session from a month later (June 12, 1925) features Jones accompanied by the St. Louis Rhythm Kings, a band of white studio musicians.

The Columbia careers of these three singers demonstrate that there was a definite marketing plan at work behind their recordings. The case of singer Monette Moore shows that Columbia did not necessarily hire all the singers they auditioned. Moore had an active recording career in the early 1920s, making numerous sides for Paramount, Vocalion, and Ajax before a single session for Columbia in October 1925, which was apparently not successful enough to warrant a contract; the fact that that it was made so late in the Classic Blues game might also have been a determining factor.

The steady sales of Bessie Smith recordings along with her frequent touring and colorful offstage life (duly reported in the black press of the time) kept her at the forefront of the Classic Blues, even after the style had begun to unravel at the midpoint of the decade. The recording formula that was obviously recognized to work for her (and Clara Smith and Maggie Jones) was to be accompanied by the young African American musicians who were playing in some of New York's best dance bands and who were at the same time conversant with the blues as an improvised, vocal-driven music. Following the April 1924 experimental sessions, Bessie Smith returned to the studios accompanied by Fletcher Henderson and one or two of his band's musicians through the summer and fall of 1924.

FLETCHER HENDERSON

At the end of June 1924, Fletcher Henderson's band had completed a run of about five months at Club Alabam. As the story (told by Don Redman) goes, in the fall of 1923, Henderson had been making a recording with a group of musicians who often worked with him in the studio when someone mentioned that the Alabam was looking for a band. On a whim, they went to the audition and played the stock arrangements they had just recorded, getting the job and launching Henderson on a career he never particularly wanted, leading a band for the next thirty years (Driggs 1979, 95).

Born in Cuthbert, Georgia, to a middle-class family, Fletcher Henderson was raised in a strict household in which both his parents were educators. He attended Atlanta University and after receiving his BS in chemistry continued to New York to begin graduate studies there. While involved in his studies, he began to moonlight as a pianist. His ability to read music fluently and also to coach singers became known and he was hired frequently to direct recording dates and also occasionally to tour. It was during a 1922 tour as the music director for Ethel Waters that he first met Louis Armstrong in New Orleans and began to absorb the new jazz style at its source, although Armstrong refused Henderson's offer to join his group at that time.

By the time he made his first recordings with Bessie Smith, Henderson was already a veteran of the recording process, having recorded more than a hundred sides with a panoply of singers as well as a dozen band instrumentals and three piano solos under his own name. By the end of 1923 he had cultivated a small circle of musicians whom he trusted to make his recording dates and play the published orchestrations then in vogue or improvise accompaniments to singers. All of these musicians were working with other bands at the time and only recorded with Henderson (and others) during the day, before their cabaret or theater jobs began.

With the stability offered by a regular residency at Club Alabam, Henderson was able to set his personnel and add to it somewhat, increasing it to ten or eleven pieces (the number of parts generally used in dance band orchestrations of the time). Two trumpets, one trombone, two or three saxes (all doubling clarinets and occasionally other woodwind instruments), piano, banjo, tuba, drums, and violin was the

standard dance band of the time. By November 1923, Henderson's
recordings were occasionally credited to "Henderson and His Club Alabam Orchestra" using a variety of instrumentation, but by the end of
January 1924, he was appearing regularly at the club with a group
including Elmer Chambers and Howard Scott (cornet), Teddy Nixon
(trombone), Don Redman and Coleman Hawkins (sax), Charlie Dixon
(banjo), Bob Escudero (tuba), Kaiser Marshall (drums), Allie Ross (violin), and himself on piano. This was apparently the personnel of the
band and the circle that Henderson drew on for recording dates for the
duration of the run at the Alabam. Henderson occasionally also used a
third sax or substituted Joe Smith for one of the cornets on recording
dates, but extant pictures of the band show the group described above.

According to Henderson's biographer Walter C. Allen, the Alabam
job ended when the club wanted Coleman Hawkins to appear as part of
the floor show without additional pay (Allen 1973, 93). This caused the
musicians to revolt and they left shortly before July 1924. Whether or
not this story is completely accurate, the band was quickly engaged to
play at the Roseland Ballroom, a much larger and more prestigious
dance hall that featured two and sometimes three bands. Although it
catered to an exclusively white clientele, the Roseland usually had one
black and one white band. By early July, the black band that had been
resident there, Armand J. Piron's Orchestra, had left to return home to
New Orleans and Henderson stepped into the job. For the next decade
or so, his band played roughly from October through May there, with
the summer months and shorter periods during the winter reserved for
tours, although the summer of 1924 was spent establishing his fan base
at the Roseland. With the benefit of a larger budget and stable base,
Henderson was able to augment the group with a third trumpet and
reed player (although the violin was dispensed with at this time).

These two additional musicians became integral parts of the black
New York jazz establishment and added a great deal of prestige to
Henderson's already influential group. With his reputation as an up-
and-coming bandleader as well as an accomplished musician, Henderson was emboldened again to attempt to hire Louis Armstrong. This
time Armstrong agreed, leaving his mentor King Oliver's band in Chicago and arriving in New York in October 1924 in time to make the band's
recording session on October 7. On Armstrong's recommendation,
Henderson also hired Buster Bailey, who was well known in Chicago as

one of the best clarinetists in the new style as well as a capable saxophone player. Both Armstrong and Bailey, along with trombonist Charlie Green (who replaced Nixon), Redman, Hawkins, and occasionally Chambers, Dixon, Escudero, and Marshall, became mainstays in the studios with the blues and cabaret singers whose recordings were still in demand.

Smith's first session after the April 1924 series began an extended association with Henderson and his Roseland musicians that continued almost uninterrupted through the fall of 1926 (although not always with Henderson himself; two sessions featured other musicians while the Henderson band was on tour) and resumed periodically through the decade. On July 22 she recorded two sides accompanied by Henderson and Don Redman, who restricted himself to playing alto sax, though with more or less the same results as the earlier sessions in which he participated. Redman was by his own admission not a great improviser and his playing tended more toward glib than passionate, making him an unsuitable partner for Smith. The next day produced two more sides of a much higher quality, with Redman replaced by Charlie Green, here making only his third or fourth recording date.

CHARLIE GREEN

Charlie Green (1895–1935) was born and raised in Omaha, Nebraska, certainly not an established center of African American blues culture, but one that somehow gave Green the tools to carve out a career as a trombonist whose specialty was generally accepted to be blues accompaniment. After many years of playing in local brass bands and a legendary territory band led by Frank "Red" Perkins (not to be confused with the white country singer Red Perkins), Green moved to New York City in 1924, joining the Henderson band in time for its opening at the Roseland in July. He was heavily featured as a soloist by Henderson, and even after Armstrong joined in the fall he was heard soloing on most of the records cut by the group until he left in the summer of 1926. After about two years of freelancing around New York he rejoined Henderson in the spring of 1928, remaining until the band broke up in the summer of 1929. After this, he played in a string of groups including bands led by Benny Carter, Elmer Snowden, Charlie Johnson, and Chick Webb before the twin ravages of tuberculosis and alcoholism combined to kill him in 1935, some accounts suggesting that he literally froze to death on his own doorstep in an alcoholic stupor.

Throughout his time in New York, Green appeared on record dozens of times in support of all the major black singers of the day: Bessie Smith, Clara Smith, Trixie Smith, Alberta Hunter, Bessie Brown, and even Ma Rainey made recordings with him either playing in a larger band or, more frequently, alone or with one or two other horns. Prior to his arrival on the scene, there were very few trombonists who were fleet enough as technicians or conversant enough in the blues tradition to fit the combined bill of playing in dance bands and accompanying singers. Green's extremely vocalized tone quality (enhanced by plunger and bucket mutes) acted as an excellent foil to the down-home blues singers he accompanied; he likely would not have been as successful with the more sophisticated styles of an Ethel Waters or Eva Taylor, although he was a good enough musician to play Henderson's notoriously difficult book as well as in pit bands for theatrical shows. Once he began recording with Bessie Smith, his trombone could be heard on perhaps a third of her subsequent sides, more than any other musician, suggesting that Smith appreciated his playing (how much input she had concerning her accompaniment is open to speculation, but presumably if she had serious objections, they would have carried weight).

WORKHOUSE BLUES

On July 23, 1924, Green and Henderson accompanied Smith on two numbers and then two more over the next two weeks. Of the four sides, "Work House Blues" (Columbia 14032-D) was the first and possibly the best. Consisting of a verse and four choruses loosely organized around the theme of female incarceration, the tune is credited to Ted Wallace, a pseudonym for Ed Kirkeby, a white musician, recording director, and publisher who was perhaps best known as Fats Waller's manager during the 1930s. Kirkeby also produced jazz recordings for Columbia during the 1920s (including many by the popular white dance band the California Ramblers), so how he was credited with "Work House Blues" (and its session mate, "House Rent Blues") is a mystery, leading one to wonder if Smith herself might have written them. Considering the fact that the subject matter is very much in the southern rural tradition, her authorship of these numbers is worth considering, as is the possibility of Green's input. He identified as part Native American, and the lyrics of the first chorus "I'm goin' to the Nation, goin' to the Territor[y]" specifically references the Oklahoma Indian territory. The other two tunes from these sessions were credited to George Brooks, which was a pseudonym for Fletcher Henderson, who was doubtless responsible for transcribing the tunes (whether or not he wrote them).

Even compared with the two tunes recorded with Redman the previous day, "Work House Blues" suggests a tremendous leap—Smith's voice has taken on a more urgent sound colored by cries and guttural rasps (for example, at the beginning of the fifth chorus: "Say he used to be mine, but look who's got him now") and a new flexibility of pitch manipulation on long notes. She also exerts a great control of the tempo, slowing the group down after the introduction and then speeding it up gradually by the end of the record, building intensity as she does.

For his part, Charlie Green demonstrates both the ability to stay out of the singer's way and also to make instrumental commentary at the end of her phrases that are both witty and occasionally profound. Answering her four repetitions of "oh, lord" on the verse, he plays a simple echo figure vocalized by his use of the plunger mute that gives the effect of a Greek chorus. As they move through the choruses, he varies his accompaniment in each chorus, with the first two being relatively simple responses that neatly dovetail with her next entrance. On the third chorus

> I wished I had a hammer of my own (x2)
> I'd give all those poor girls a long old happy home

he changes his approach to long-held notes, creating a chorale-like feel not far removed from a church hymn (not counting the lyrics, of course). On the final chorus he plays more active fills at the end of the lines, with both trombone and singer apparently igniting each other and ending with a bold major ninth, unusual at the time.

LOUIS ARMSTRONG

By the time Louis Armstrong (1901–1971) arrived in New York to join Fletcher Henderson's Orchestra as its third trumpet player, he was already regarded both in his hometown of New Orleans and his adopted city of Chicago as being on the cutting edge of jazz. Armstrong was born to a single mother in the poorest section of New Orleans where sustaining life was a constant struggle. After a youthful contretemps with the law (he was arrested after shooting a gun in celebration of New Year's Eve in 1912), he was remanded to the Colored Waifs Home, a halfway house for wayward boys. It was there that he was given his first musical instruction, first playing baritone horn and then cornet in the school band. Released in June 1914, Armstrong never returned to school, instead making a living of sorts at a succession of menial jobs while continuing to play music.

Local musicians quickly realized that the young Armstrong was uniquely gifted and began hiring him. The top cornet player in New Orleans in the late 1910s was Joe "King" Oliver, who took Armstrong under his wing and gave him tips, enabling him to begin playing with better groups. By 1919 he had progressed enough as a musician to join Fate Marable's band, playing on the legendary river cruises on the Mississippi River during the summers, a job that required the ability to read music as well as to improvise. Marable was an exacting bandleader and Armstrong learned a great deal about music as well as the professional side of the business during this three summers on the riverboats.

In August 1922 Armstrong left New Orleans for good to join Oliver in Chicago. The older player had moved there several years earlier and established himself as the leader of one of the best dance bands in the city. Calling it his "Creole Jazz Band," Oliver recalled some of the New Orleans culture with which he and all but one of the musicians in the group had grown up. Armstrong, Oliver, and the Dodds brothers (clarinetist Johnny and drummer Baby) were not Creoles—they were from the lower economic and cultural bracket that was simply identified as "black" and as such were much more conversant in vernacular African American musical practices such as blues than were the "uptown" Creoles in New Orleans. This group played at both the Lincoln and Royal Gardens in Chicago until 1924 and made a series of what were among the first recordings by a black jazz band.

By late 1924 the original band had gradually disintegrated and Armstrong had married pianist Lillian Hardin, the only non–New Orleansian in the band. Hardin must be given credit for encouraging (some would say bullying) her husband into advancing his career. As a well-schooled musician, she furthered his musical education in terms of reading music and composing his own songs. She also pushed him into accepting Fletcher Henderson's offer to go to New York in the summer of 1925, leaving Oliver. By this point, Armstrong was a good musician as far as reading and technique were concerned—vital requirements for playing with top dance bands in the 1920s. One wonders what he was reading, though—published arrangements of the period included only two trumpet parts, so Armstrong might have been hired initially to play solos, although someone of his ability would have had no trouble inventing a third part in the arrangements.

The incredibly fresh and innovative way Armstrong played cornet has already been commented on, but many musicians have left accounts of how all the musicians in New York made pilgrimages to the Roseland whenever possible to hear the new style and approach. Henderson's frequent recordings with his band almost invariably showcase Armstrong and these recordings became influential throughout the country, supported by tours the band made throughout the northeast during the year he spent with the group. In addition to the recordings he made with Henderson and Bessie Smith, Armstrong recorded dozens of songs behind Ma Rainey, Trixie Smith, Clara Smith, Maggie Jones, and others as well as in small jazz groups led by Clarence Williams and Perry Bradford. His unique combination of abilities as an improviser, reader, and seasoned dance band musician put him in incredible demand during his whole time in New York.

RECKLESS BLUES

One of the first tunes that Armstrong recorded with Bessie Smith was "Reckless Blues" (January 14, 1925, Columbia 14056-D), a straight-ahead performance of four blues choruses. Beginning with a four-bar instrumental introduction establishing the sound spectrum of the plunger-muted and highly vocalized cornet supported by Fred Longshaw's harmonium (a small reed organ), Smith enters with some of the most passionate singing of her recording career to that point. The funereal tempo of the piece (accentuated by the harmonium, which was often used in small churches) allows the singer time to stretch her phrases and bend her notes to create a real sense of communion with the lyrics.

The record gives credit to Longshaw as the composer, but as with some of Smith's earlier recordings, one suspects that she was the author of the lyrics, even if she didn't notate the music. The progress of the four verses is not absolutely narrative or thematic, but they do revolve around the romantic habits of the singer. The last verse,

> Daddy, Mama wants some lovin'—Daddy, Mama wants some huggin'
> Darn it pretty papa, Mama wants some lovin' I vow
> Darn it pretty papa, Mama wants some lovin' right now

changes the AAB lyric structure of the blues a bit but rounds out the feelings contained in the progression of the verses.

For his part, Armstrong does what he was acknowledged by many to do better than anyone else at the time—accompany singers in the "down-home" blues idiom. His note choice, timing, and pitch manipulation are equal to Smith's own, and the two create a synergy that was almost completely unknown on record at the time—the only previous examples being Armstrong and Sidney Bechet locking horns on some of Clarence Williams's recordings from the previous month. Using a plunger mute (which he largely abandoned after the middle 1920s), the cornetist matches the singer's pitch bend for bend and dovetails his phrases with hers, staying out of the way for the most part. Although Longshaw's instrumental contribution here (and on "St. Louis Blues," which is discussed in chapter 7) is generally dismissed, the limited possibilities of the harmonium actually free up the other performers in a way that prevents the conflict that one can hear between Armstrong and Smith on the three tunes recorded that day on which Longshaw plays a "busier" piano accompaniment.

I AIN'T GONNA PLAY NO SECOND FIDDLE

The final recorded collaboration between Armstrong and Smith (Columbia 14090-D, May 27, 1925) was a tune by Perry Bradford that was presumably done for a specific singer or show, but no information exists as for whom or what it was intended. Armstrong, Green, and Henderson back Smith on a performance that was almost exclusively vocal—the cornet player's discretion (not always noted on his recordings accompanying singers) is here forced, with virtually no pauses in the vocal line for the extent of the record.

The song begins with a verse sung by a woman lamenting her mistreatment at the hands of her man and her resolve to assert herself. This resolve becomes a declaration in the chorus, which begins with the song's title. The structure of the chorus is unusual (and may account for its relative lack of popularity on record during the 1920s). It is a long form—thirty-two bars—but in an older ABAC form that was more common to marches and instrumental music than vocal tunes. The first half of the section I am calling "C" is in fact identical in structure and usage to the "B" section of many sixteen-bar AABA tunes from the period (see the discussion of "Baby Doll" later). It was used as a kind of climax to the narrative of the lyrics of these tunes and often expressed the singer's defiance through humor or hyperbole. In "I Ain't Gonna Play No Second Fiddle," it happens four times—once in the form of the chorus and then three more times as a coda (followed by the last four bars of the tune, restating the song title and main theme). Smith's lyrics for these three subsections are set in relief even more by the musicians playing stop-time (playing only the first beat of each of the four measures while the singer continues). The first three of her lyrics:

I called to your house the other night, caught you and your good gal havin' a fight
I caught you with your good-time vamp, so, now papa I'm gonna put out your lamp
Oh, poppa, I ain't sore, you ain't gonna mess up with me no more

In performance, one could imagine the singer doing many more variations on this theme and continuing the stop-time section (sometimes called a "patter") indefinitely, depending on the amusement of the audience.

The performance of this song is fairly casual—while Armstrong occasionally asserts himself, Green is almost completely subdued after the instrumental introduction and seems content to play very short comments and held notes. Henderson's playing is merely supportive, staying out of the way and allowing the brass players to supply what little variation there is. One wonders if Frank Walker made the decision at this point that Smith needed a different sound in her accompaniment and decreed that Henderson use Joe Smith (the new addition to his band's trumpet section) on further recordings or if Henderson himself made that decision. Although Smith's next three recording sessions were accompanied by non-Henderson musicians (his band being on tour throughout the summer before returning to the Roseland in October 1925), her sessions beginning in November and continuing through 1926 featured Henderson's men with the exception of two: one in December 1925 featured two members of her touring group, Longshaw and cornetist Shelton Hemphill, and one in March 1926 used Clarence Williams while Henderson was touring the Midwest.

JOE SMITH

Joe Smith (1902–1937) was raised in a family of trumpet and cornet players. In addition to his elder brother Russell—one of the most respected lead trumpeters from the 1920s through the 1940s who played with James Reese Europe, Fletcher Henderson, Noble Sissle, Benny Carter, and Cab Calloway's bands among many others—four other brothers and his father were all brass players in Ripley, Ohio. Joe Smith came to New York around 1920 and quickly established himself as a technically accomplished player (although according to Henderson he was never a great reader) who was also a fine soloist and accompanist. Unlike the dominant style of playing among black jazz brass players in New York at the time, Smith played with a large, round sound that did not depend extensively on mutes to create tonal variety. He was a well-trained technician who could fit into a dance band section as well as improvise, and his tone was sweet without being cloying, an important part of why he was regarded as perhaps the top trumpet/cornet player in black bands immediately before Louis Armstrong's arrival.

Smith did not join Henderson's band as a full-time member until April 1925, although he appeared numerous times on recordings with the pianist, especially behind singers. Before joining the band, Smith had appeared in several stage shows including *In Bamville*, later called *The Chocolate Dandies*, in which Smith was appearing when he first heard Armstrong early in 1925. Clearly, Henderson regarded his talents highly—he used him on recording dates although he wasn't a regular with his band and divided both the solo work and the outside recording dates with Armstrong after they were both members. Some rivalry apparently existed between the two cornetists, at least in the eyes of the press and some fans, but there was no apparent animosity between the two men.

By the time he made his first recording with Bessie Smith, Joe Smith had already made recordings with a dozen other singers as well as deputizing on a couple of dates with the Henderson band. The first date uniting the Smiths resulted in two vaudeville-type songs with blues influence and also included Green. The nature of the songs ("Weeping Willow Blues" and "Bye Bye Blues") was such that very little scope was given to the horn players. In any event, the cornetist disappears from the recording studios for the next seven months, perhaps while he was touring with *The Chocolate Dandies*.

After joining Henderson in April 1925, Smith begins appearing with great frequency on outside recording dates run by the pianist. Over the course of the summer he recorded with Bessie Smith, Maggie Jones, Leola Wilson, and Ethel Waters. At the same time, Louis Armstrong also did recordings with Bessie Smith and Leola Wilson, but the frequency of his outside dates with Henderson diminished greatly, suggesting that Henderson (and perhaps the singers) preferred the more subtle sounds of Smith. Most notably, Smith was given the nod to play the lead in the band backing Bessie Smith and Maggie Jones on the experimental electric recording session on May 5 and 6, 1925 (see chapter 2 for a discussion of "Yellow Dog Blues").

CAKE WALKIN' BABIES FROM HOME

"Cake Walkin' Babies from Home" (Columbia 35673, May 5, 1925—it remained unreleased until 1940 and does not have a number in the 14000 series) was a popular tune credited to Clarence Williams, Henry Troy, and Chris Smith (not Bessie, as is sometimes claimed) that harkened back to the ragtime era when cakewalks were a popular form of social event that rewarded superior dancing with cake—a tradition that may have gone back to slavery. Troy and Smith were both black minstrel and vaudeville performers whose careers went back to the early years of the century and were probably the main songwriters, with

Williams adding his name as publisher's prerogative. Accompanied by Henderson's Hot Six including Joe Smith, Green, Coleman Hawkins (on clarinet), Henderson, Charlie Dixon, and Ralph Escudero, Smith turns "Cake Walkin' Babies" into a much more modern-sounding tune than its antecedents would suggest. The new clarity made possible by the electric recording process probably encouraged Columbia to increase the size of the backing group, although it was clearly a casual musical setting (really just a New Orleans/Dixieland–style performance behind the singer—the Jones sides made the same day were more organized and obviously had some written parts for the band). Bessie Smith nevertheless sings with a command and a rhythmic energy that is now much easier to appreciate. This was also the recording that figured into the famous story of the tent—the Columbia engineers had apparently rigged up a canvas tent in the studio to act as an acoustic control for this unfamiliar process and at some point the whole thing collapsed on top of the performers, creating pandemonium and some choice salty remarks from the singer, as well as postponement of the other tune for the session ("Yellow Dog Blues" discussed in chapter 2) until the next day.

Although in some senses this performance harkens back to minstrel days, Smith gives what might be a better indication here of what she must have sounded like in person in front of a jazz band on the tent show circuit as opposed to just a piano in a theater. Sounding in some ways like old-style singers like Sophie Tucker, Smith demonstrates much greater pitch control and flexibility than the earlier stylists, and clearly dominates the performance in terms of tempo and feeling more than practically any singer of the day. Her "shouting" delivery here does not detract from the expressiveness of her singing, which foregrounds rhythmic propulsion more than did any previous singers, clearly showing what attracted contemporary jazz musicians and singers as well as those of future generations. It is curious why this performance was unreleased (and why, unlike all her other rejected recordings, was saved in Columbia's vaults). Was the tune considered too old fashioned or was the performance perhaps too stylistically advanced to appeal to Smith's fan base?

BABY DOLL

Far more interesting from the point of view of the accompaniment is "Baby Doll" (May 4, 1926, Columbia 14147-D). This session features just the two Smiths and Henderson and was extremely well recorded (clearly, the year that had elapsed between "Cake Walkin' Babies" and this was put to good use by Columbia's engineers) and demonstrates their interaction well. The introduction features the cornetist's huge, open sound and lyrical approach, which he continues behind the vocal.

The usual verse sets the scene of a woman with heartache, not because she lost her man, but because she never had one and was lonely. Included here is a reference to what several commentators hear as "Cuban Doll," which I find a little difficult to understand. If that is indeed the lyric, it might make sense, given that a Cuban doll apparently had voodoo or occult associations that would go along with the later lyric referencing a gypsy fortune-teller.

The chorus of this song is in a sixteen bar, AABA form, which was considerably more common than the better known thirty-two bar Tin Pan Alley AABA form that was developing through the 1920s, particularly among Broadway and show composers. This shorter form (the chorus of "Baby Doll" is actually eighteen bars—each chorus contains a two-bar turnaround at the end) had been a staple of the repertoire of singers from at least the 1910s and may have its antecedents in the nineteenth century. Generally, the "A" sections are lyrically similar, while the "B" section is entirely different, with the number of choruses performed by the singer dependent on the variety of lyrics to this section. Jazz players occasionally refer to this form as the "Jada" or "How Come You Do Me Like You Do" form (in later jazz styles it is referred to as the "Doxy" changes). Smith had recorded many songs in this form, including "Beale Street Mama" and "Aggravatin' Papa," among many others. Often, the lyrics to the middle section are further highlighted by the accompaniment playing stop-time, as they do on both choruses here, with Smith singing. Here, the "B" sections provide the contrast and probably the onstage humor when Smith sings

[First chorus] He can be ugly, he can be black, so long as he can Eagle Rock and Ball the Jack
[Second chorus] Lawd, I went to the gypsy to get my fortune told, she said you in hard luck Bessie, doggone your bad luck soul

The first chorus refers to contemporary and slightly earlier dances in popular culture, which also were sometimes used as euphemisms for sexual activity (as they are here). The first "AA" of the second chorus is given over to a cornet solo that demonstrates Joe Smith's tone and relaxed approach, using figuration that decorates the melody rather than completely recasting it, as we have seen with Louis Armstrong.

"Baby Doll" is credited to Bessie Smith and "H. Webman," of whom nothing is known (one wonders if he was the same Hal Webman who was an editor and blues columnist for *Downbeat* and *Billboard* magazines in the 1940s and 1950s). With references to superstition, interracial prejudice, and overt sexuality, this song represents a direct link to rural African American popular culture and also presents an artistically compelling if somewhat sanitized preview of the sort of material Smith was to focus on during the last two years of the decade.

The recorded evidence seems to give credence to the idea that Joe Smith was Bessie Smith's favorite accompanist; reminiscences by Ruby Walker (discussed in the next chapter) and trumpeter Demas Dean (Albertson 2003, 164) bear this out.

BUSTER BAILEY

William C. "Buster" Bailey (1902–1967) had one of the longest and most consistent careers of any black jazz musician of his era. Born in Memphis, he began playing clarinet very early and showed enough aptitude to join W. C. Handy's band as a teenager in 1917. By 1919 he had settled in Chicago where he began formal clarinet study with Franz Schoepp, who also taught Benny Goodman at the same time. During that period he was with Erskine Tate's Vendome Orchestra playing a variety of light classical and theater music on saxophone as well as clarinet before joining King Oliver's Creole Jazz Band at the end of 1923. Here he played alongside Louis Armstrong until Armstrong left for New York the following October. Acting on the trumpet player's recommendation, Henderson sent for Bailey, who arrived in time to make recording sessions with the band in the middle of October 1924 and almost immediately established himself as the best jazz clarinet player in the city. His fluency as an improviser and his extensive formal training enabled him to function in a wide variety of settings, from the most casual blues accompaniment to classical ensembles, keeping him busy for the rest of his life in a countless groups including long stays with Henderson (1924–1929, 1934, 1936–1937), Noble Sissle (1929–1930, 1931–1933), John Kirby (1937–1946), Red Allen's band at the Metropole (much of the 1950s), and Armstrong's All-Stars (1965–1967). In addition to his regular employment, Bailey made hundreds of casual recording sessions from 1924 until shortly before his death and was highly regarded for his professionalism and ability to adapt to practically any musical circumstance.

JAZZBO BROWN FROM MEMPHIS TOWN

"Jazzbo Brown from Memphis Town" (Columbia 14133-D, March 18, 1926) is a mysterious tune. Credited to "Brooks," the tune was not recorded by anyone but Bessie Smith during the 1920s. In fact, "George Brooks" was a pseudonym for Fletcher Henderson, who with Buster Bailey accompanies Smith on this session. Henderson was not really known as a songwriter, although he is credited as composer on a number of Smith's records under both names. A few isolated examples of this can be found in 1923 and 1924, but "Jazzbo Brown" begins a series of ten recordings made between March and October 1926 made with Henderson where the pianist was given composer credit on half. One wonders if this was some kind of profit-sharing plan to entice him into being the recording director for the notoriously difficult singer. He evidently was responsible as music director for writing the melody and chords and then copyrighting the song, although it seems difficult to believe that he also wrote the lyrics to all the tunes attributed to him. It is possible that Smith was responsible for the lyrics, which may or may not have had common-stock folk origins—Bailey himself confirmed that Brooks and Henderson were the same person and that Smith often did write the lyrics to those tunes (Shapiro and Hentoff 1955, 244–45).

As a historical figure, Jazzbo Brown (or a variant of the spelling) was supposed to have been a blues musician, perhaps from the Mississippi Delta, whose name might have been appropriated for the new music. George Gershwin even uses him as a piano-playing character in the first act of *Porgy and Bess* (1934) to set the scene in Catfish Row. Singers Ollie Powers, Mamie Smith, and Roy Evans recorded songs about similar characters using similar imagery during the 1920s. The character in Bessie Smith's version is a "clarinet-playing hound," who "ain't seen no music school, he can't read a note" but "wraps his big fat lips 'round that doggone horn" and outplays trained players who play "classic stuff, like them Hoffman's tales." The Paul Bunyanesque approach to this story takes on a more familiar southern folk flavor with the lyric "when he blows and pats his feet, makes a butcher leave his meat," variations of which can be found in many blues and black vaudeville songs.

The song itself begins with the inevitable verse introducing Jazzbo and then goes into a thirty-two-bar chorus in the older, march trio (ABAC) style, which by 1926 had been largely forsaken in favor of the newer AABA structure. Henderson and Bailey begin with a suitably strutting introduction featuring the clarinet playing some yelping figures that one suspects were a nod more to the topic of the song than an attempt to play jazz or blues. Bailey, though having his instrument and hometown in common with Jazzbo, was in no way self-taught or a limited musician. From the beginning of the vocal, the tempo begins to accelerate, which was atypical on Smith's recordings. Typically she favored slower tempos and many examples can be heard of her dragging the tempo down after an instrumental introduction that was obviously faster than she wanted. Bailey's own testimony was that she preferred slow tempos on recordings and in general. The clarinet playing on this tune (and its session mate, "Gin House Blues") tends toward shrill, though it certainly benefits from a great deal more technical flexibility and stylistic understanding than had Smith's previous clarinet accompanists. His solo on the first half of the second chorus continues the story of Jazzbo, exploring the high register and foregrounding a fast vibrato that was common among reed players in the 1920s. For his background figures behind Smith, Bailey has the discretion to restrict himself mainly to the middle register and in general to stay out of her way.

ONE AND TWO BLUES

Bessie Smith and Her Blue Boys are credited with "One and Two Blues" (Columbia 14172-D, October 26, 1926), made after the Henderson band returned from its summer tour and started up again at the Roseland. The song is once again credited to George Brooks, but the same conclusions can be drawn as with "Jazzbo Brown": that this was a tune invented by Smith and transcribed by Henderson. Again in sixteen-bar AABA form (despite its title), the tune begins with a verse and then a vocal chorus followed by the two "A" sections played by the Blue Boys. Smith comes back in on the "B" section, then sings an additional "B" section before finishing with the final "A." This bit of structural manipulation was probably common onstage when songs like this were used to feature singers. The three "B" sections she sings:

If you want me to love you—heap much, let mama feel that money touch
Quit messin' around—you'll hear what I say start in to bringin' eight hours a day
If you must be a rat—here's a fact be a long-tailed one, have plenty of jack

enlarge on the theme of the song, which is that the man in question is out of touch with what things cost in the city (he is a country boy, apparently) and the singer in the last line winds up with the title lyric. Probably intended as a comic number on the stage, "One and Two Blues" comments on the age-old conflict between love and money—a conflict Smith knew intimately at the time, given the state of her marriage. The Blue Boys were made up of Henderson, Joe Smith, and Buster Bailey. From the beginning of the record, the sound is more refined and in general more organized than many of Bessie Smith's recordings from the period. The cornet and clarinet voicing on the introduction was clearly worked out in advance, if not written out by Henderson. Although the level of improvisation behind the vocal is not particularly high, Joe Smith in particular continues to show that his taste and discretion matched with his rich tone were an excellent foil for the singer. Bailey, on the other hand, does not show up terribly well here; his background playing is somewhat aimless, consisting primarily of long notes, and his part in the sixteen-bar instrumental interlude becomes quite shrill in its ascent into the upper register. The general impression is of musical efficiency rather than any real commitment to the proceedings, which marked many of Bessie Smith's recordings for the next few years.

5

A GOOD MAN IS HARD TO FIND

By 1927 Bessie Smith was one of the most highly paid and successful black entertainers in the world. She regularly toured the Theatre Owner's Booking Agents (TOBA) theater circuit throughout the northeast, Midwest, and Gulf Coast region as well as the southeastern part of the United States, where she had spent much of her early career. She was no longer a single, appearing with whatever local musicians or shows were appearing, but a headliner carrying her own company with her. At their peak, the Bessie Smith shows featured as many as a dozen chorus girls who would do dance specialties alone as well as together, a male dancer or group, a comedian, and often another female singer who would specialize in popular numbers, whereas Smith performed blues and folk material. For at least part of this period, her brother Clarence and nephew T. J. Hill functioned as road managers and possibly masters of ceremonies during her shows. Although press mentions of her earlier tours usually cite only a pianist as her accompaniment, later shows had bands of five or six pieces accompanying Smith and the other performers. During her 1927 tour, she even bought her own railroad car to ease transportation headaches and probably to combat the racism black performers routinely experienced on the road.

After Smith's recording career began, Frank Walker apparently took some hand in arranging tours of her company, suggesting that her work outside the studio was closely tied to her work in it. Numerous accounts exist of members of her companies selling her Columbia records during performances, leading to the conclusion that this merchandising was a significant part of her revenue stream during the tours—whether she purchased copies to resell or was given them as part of Walker's promotional schemes is unknown. Indeed the publicity of having such a long series of recordings on Columbia with its international distribution helped to ensure that her tours were invariably well attended even after her recording career began to tail off in the late 1920s, and the recording industry itself bottomed out in the Depression.

The general pattern of Smith's touring career changed as the years passed, but there was usually some kind of extended summer tent show tour (called "Bessie Smith's Harlem Frolics" or some variation of that name beginning in the summer of 1926 and continuing with some interruptions thereafter) through the South and then a TOBA theater tour in the winter and early spring. These theater tours took her up and down the East Coast and as far west as New Orleans and Chattanooga but rarely beyond that—there seems to be no evidence of any Bessie Smith show going to the West Coast or even the upper Midwest. Her fan base remained solidly among rural southern blacks, although transplanted African American communities in northern cities (especially Chicago) also greeted her appearances enthusiastically. It is significant that even at the height of her popularity she refused to live in New York City fulltime. She maintained a home in Philadelphia from 1921 until her death and apparently found the less hectic life there more conducive to her idea of peace and quiet when not on tour.

The financial and popular success that Smith had found by the middle 1920s translated into many headaches for her. Although she had her brother as the paymaster and tour manager and sometimes her nephew and husband along as well, she was the star of the show, and she also assumed much responsibility for booking, repertoire, discipline, and so on. Her power along with the discretionary income she now had also translated into a catalog of personal excess that, amazingly, did not seem to slow her progress as a businessperson or artist. The main source we have for the events of some of these tours and the behavior of the star is Ruby Walker, a niece of Smith's husband Jack Gee.

RUBY WALKER

Ruby Walker (1903–1977) had first met Bessie during a trip to Philadelphia, although this was apparently before Jack Gee came into the picture. Ruby was his niece, although the exact familial connection is difficult to determine from existing records. She claimed to be present at the house of her grandmother (Gee's mother) at the time shortly before Smith's first successful recording session when the not-yet-married couple was staying there in order to rehearse with Clarence Williams. Smith's singing instantly captivated Walker, who devoted the rest of her life to the memory of Smith, even changing her name to "Ruby Smith" in the late 1930s and adopting some of the older singer's repertoire for her own singing career.

In addition to imitating some of Smith's vocal mannerisms, Walker also went on tour with her beginning in the spring of 1924. It is her extensive reminiscences that form the core of what we know about the personality and habits of Bessie Smith on both a personal and professional level. Smith apparently took on the younger Walker as a traveling companion and running buddy in addition to using her in the chorus lines of numerous shows for the next several seasons. Walker gives a continuous account of how the marriage between Gee and Smith began to go bad, especially after he tried to act as a road manager for her show, a task Walker felt the marginally educated Gee was not up to. According to her, it was Frank Walker who served as the booker for Smith's touring company while her brother and nephew oversaw the day-to-day operation of the touring company. Gee would occasionally travel with the group, creating a great deal of resentment as well as tension between the couple, and the explosive fights recalled by Walker and other family members often started over incidents on these tours.

When Gee was present, Smith's outward behavior was reasonably restrained and decorous, but his departure invariably triggered her abandonment of conservative tendencies, and Walker's accounts of their adventures sharing men and women, drinking binges, and a legendary visit to a Detroit "buffet flat" (essentially a sex show run for the benefit of visiting black entertainers and Pullman porters) are not titillating so much as pornographic. Several stories have violent endings, such as when Walker was shot in the foot after an altercation in an after-hours club (Albertson 2003, 58) or when Smith was stabbed by a man who was attempting to take advantage of one of the chorus girls (Albertson 2003, 93).

Walker's stories were remarkably detailed, and she clearly had intimate knowledge of Smith both on- and offstage, but some of the stories simply do not chronologically add up. Apart from her claim to have been a witness to the rehearsal for Smith's first recording session (which must have occurred either before she met Gee or while he was in the hospital), Albertson states that Walker was twenty years Smith's junior (Albertson 2003, 71), but various online sources cite her birth year as 1903, making her less than ten years younger. That date seems to make more sense. If she had been born in, say, 1913, she would have been only eleven when she made her first tour, an unlikely prospect. In her reminiscences, Walker also mentions her disappointment that she was not allowed to go on the spring 1925 tour because she and her friend Lillian Simpson were still in school, also an unlikely scenario if they were in their early twenties. Walker's exact relationship with the Gees is also murky: her mother is listed as Parthenia Lundy (Jack Gee's half sister), who was born in 1883, which is at variance with Walker's claim that her mother was in her late forties when she was born. Her story about Smith being shot in an after-hours club in Baltimore Albertson dates as December 1923, before she was a regular on Smith's tours and raising questions both of memory and veracity.

Nevertheless, Walker's interviews are consistent in their portrayal of Smith as a larger-than-life figure of immense appetites and abilities. Small details such as Smith's preference for Joe Smith over Armstrong as an accompanist (even to the point of bringing her records with Smith along on tour to demonstrate to her touring musicians what she wanted) are illuminating, even if some things should be taken with a grain of salt. Some of her stories can be corroborated by contemporary newspaper references, such as the occasion in Chattanooga in March 1925, when Smith was stabbed after beating up a drunk who was bothering Walker and some of the other girls in the show.

The 1925 summer tent show tour was significant in that it debuted a custom-made railroad car for the troupe. Now, traveling through the segregated and often violent South was a great deal easier, and it encouraged Frank Walker to organize much more extensive tours. Ruby Walker recalled this tour and several of its violent and booze-fueled events in detail, although, curiously, she is not mentioned by name in the extensive review of the show in the *Chicago Defender*, which lists all members of the cast, including the band and the promoters (Albertson 2003, 106). This was perhaps before she joined the tour, although once again chronology is unclear.

There was clearly some rivalry between the two women, at least in Walker's eyes. In addition to battling Smith over at least one man on the early tours, Walker also had designs on a singing career—her attendance at the October 25, 1925, recording session led to a near-violent confrontation with Smith, who heard Ruby Walker approach Frank Walker about making a recording of her own. Walker's friend Lillian Simpson joined the tour at some point in 1926 and almost immediately began a romantic relationship with Smith that became almost as contentious as Smith's relationship with Gee. The affair ended with Simpson being sent away after a failed suicide attempt. An affair with another one of the chorus line in early 1927 was interrupted by a surprise visit by Gee, who probably saw this as the death knell of the marriage—after this, the domestic arrangements between Gee and Smith were basically severed.

The other significant personal reminiscence about Smith's life and career during the 1920s came from her sister-in-law Maud (Clarence's wife), who toured occasionally with the shows, but was more involved with the family in Philadelphia. Maud's stories occasionally paralleled Walker's (concerning, for example, some of the violent confrontations and affairs that occurred with such frequency in Smith's life) but in general presented a more balanced account of her domestic existence. Although she did not have a high regard for Jack Gee, Maud was more charitable toward him than was Walker and seemed to feel that Smith played him against the other members of her family (particularly her sister Viola) in order to maintain some kind of power over them. When Richard Morgan came into Smith's romantic life in the early 1930s, Maud was highly positive about their relationship while Walker was very negative, suggesting the extent to which the two formerly close friends had drifted apart (see chapter 6).

Even with increasing turmoil in her personal life, Smith's career continued to accelerate through the middle 1920s, spurred on in no small degree by the success and frequency of her recordings. The increasing demand for both Smith and the Henderson band for tours and personal appearances made their collaboration on records more difficult, and the singer often had other accompanists during this period. Given the level of musicianship to which buyers of Bessie Smith records had become accustomed, most of these are considered to be subpar, with one significant exception.

JAMES P. JOHNSON

James P. Johnson (1894–1955) is considered to be the dean of the Harlem stride piano style. Born in New Jersey, he moved with his family to New York by the time he was twelve. There he became an enthusiastic consumer of the urban black music scene. Influenced by church music (his mother was a singer and pianist), classical music, and ragtime, Johnson became an accomplished self-taught pianist and was playing professionally by the time he was eighteen. Realizing the need for more formal training, he studied classically for several years until his early twenties, learning how to write and arrange music as well as developing an imposing piano technique. Johnson began his recording career in the late 1910s doing piano rolls of his compositions and other popular songs, and the results, while showing a definite ragtime influence (as well as a knowledge of transitional pianists such as Eubie Blake and Luckey Roberts), pointed toward a new and more flexible rhythmic feel. His "Carolina Shout," which he first recorded on a piano roll in 1918, became one of the great test pieces of the genre, featuring the characteristic "striding" bass lines as well as the heavily syncopated melody and continually moving chord progression in a multistrain arrangement.

By the early 1920s, Johnson had begun composing music for the stage, including the successful 1923 Broadway show *Runnin' Wild*, which produced the hit song "Charleston" and led to a string of popular songs rivaled only by his sometime student, Fats Waller. By the time he began recording with Bessie Smith in February 1927, Johnson was considered the finest pianist in New York and made dozens of recordings under his own name as well as with Trixie Smith, Lavinia Tuner, Perry Bradford, and he would later record with Ethel Waters, who cited him as her favorite accompanist. Johnson and Smith's careers were intertwined from that period until her recording session of June 9, 1930, and included her single film appearance (discussed in chapter 7), for which

Johnson led the band and arranged much of the music. Following this, Johnson anticipated the diminution of playing opportunities during the Depression by devoting himself to study and the composition of more classical works including his tone poem "Yamekraw," which was presented at Carnegie Hall in 1928, and culminating in a single performance of the "blues opera" *De Organizer* that he composed to a libretto by Langston Hughes in 1940.

During the late 1920s Johnson was busy writing and performing for various musicals and theatrical shows in New York (including *Keep Shufflin'* in 1928 and *Messin' Around* in 1929) and accompanying singers on record and providing songs for other productions. Generally considered to be the best accompanist in the business, Johnson approached the piano in orchestral terms and provided both the standard rhythmic and harmonic underpinning for a singer (as had Henderson and Clarence Williams, with varying degrees of success) but also an interactive component normally provided by a horn player. It is significant that in her twelve recordings with Johnson (not counting the film or her two gospel recordings), Smith did not try to fill up the spaces at the end of her vocal phrases the way she often did on other records she made accompanied only by a pianist. Clearly, she respected his abilities and was content to allow him to musically comment on her vocal lines.

Johnson was truly an orchestral pianist—his technique and imagination allowed him to create an accompaniment for a singer that went far beyond the efforts of practically any other pianist of the day. Clarence Williams was a mediocre piano player at best with very limited technique and was generally able only to re-create the most elemental "boom-chick" type of background figures, often getting into trouble when he tried to introduce more complexity. Fletcher Henderson was a very good technician but not a terribly flexible or inspired improviser, so his framing of the vocal lines was static, if competent. Some of Smith's regular touring accompanists such as Irving Johns, Fred Longshaw, and Porter Grainger were generally better but again not terribly inspired or inspiring in the more modern concept of jazz piano.

Johnson, on the other hand, specialized both in composing and arranging songs and backing singers. At the same time he was a brilliant improviser who was clearly reluctant to repeat any formula or revert to mere clichés behind a singer (or an instrumental soloist, for that matter). Although Smith left no comments about Johnson, her contemporary Ethel Waters (who was notoriously stingy with praise) raved about his style accompanying her on records and on his contributions to music in general (Shapiro and Hentoff 1955, 176). The recordings by both Waters and Smith on which Johnson is the sole accompanist rank among the best of each.

Johnson and Smith had doubtless known each other and probably performed together at various points before their first recording together. Johnson's wife Mae Wright recalled seeing Smith perform in Atlanta as early as 1920, when she and her husband were touring with a different company, and both the singer and pianist were well enough known in their professions that their paths presumably crossed frequently. For some reason, Johnson was engaged to accompany Smith on two sessions in the late winter and early spring of 1927, sandwiching two sessions with Henderson and his musicians. For these sessions there were no instruments other than piano behind Smith, and for the first time there is really no letdown of musical intensity with no horn player to fill in at the ends of the vocal phrases.

PREACHIN' THE BLUES/BACKWATER BLUES

For the first recorded collaboration of Johnson and Smith (February 17, 1927), two tunes credited to the singer were performed. The first was a strangely constructed comic tune that combines blues and religious themes in a way that presages her final date with Johnson and the Bessemer Singers in 1930 (discussed in chapter 2). The second was an elemental blues with lyrics inspired by difficulties Smith experienced on tour several times.

During her autumn 1927 tent show tour, Smith and her company experienced a fact of life for entertainers touring the small towns of the South. A local flood made it necessary to abandon the railroad car at one point and take rowboats to the next town, where the distress of the local population caused her to create blues lyrics commemorating the difficulties. Maud Smith remembered Smith sitting at her kitchen table in Philadelphia when she returned from the tour writing the lyrics to "Backwater Blues" (Columbia 14195-D).

Structurally, this song is just a short piano introduction and coda sandwiching seven blues choruses, which, somewhat unusually for Classic Blues, is roughly narrative and thematically organized. Often, blues tunes from the 1920s (whether Classic Blues or the male-dominated Country Blues style mentioned in chapter 6) were simply collections of blues phrases and images combined with little regard for narrative structure or any type of story. The idea of "telling a story" was more common to folk ballads and even popular Tin Pan Alley tunes of an earlier vintage. "Backwater Blues," on the other hand, presents the singer's experience dealing with one of the regular river floods in the Delta region, which were chiefly punishing to those (usually African American) people who inhabited the backwater, or low-lying regions that were most susceptible to flooding.

If Smith wrote these lyrics in response to what she had seen on tour in the fall of 1926, her timing was impeccable—"Backwater Blues" was released in early March 1927, and the worst of the disastrous Mississippi flood occurred the following month, making Smith and Johnson's recording especially poignant and popular. Her third chorus,

> Then they rowed a little boat about five miles 'cross the pond
> Then they rowed a little boat about five miles 'cross the pond
> I packed all my clothes, throwed them in and they rowed me along

must have been particularly resonant to those who had lost everything in the tragedy. The final chorus, in which she does a combination of humming and moaning in the first eight bars, is an intensification of those feelings that she had established in the first seven verses.

For his part, Johnson immediately sets the mood with a rolling, almost boogie-woogie bass line in the introduction that he continues through the fourth chorus. On the fourth chorus he adapts that line into a descending chromatic pattern that calls to mind Jimmy Yancey's slightly later blues piano piece, "Yancey Special." He continues variations of the rolling bass until the coda when he momentarily switches into a more typical stride pattern. Although boogie-woogie can often be a relentless, repetitive music due to its insistent and relatively invariable bass pattern, Johnson here changes his figures and the balance between his left and right hand interaction between each chorus, spurring Smith to some of the most impassioned singing of her recorded career.

"Preachin' the Blues" (Columbia 14195-D) is another Smith composition that references drinking under a viaduct in Atlanta (where, for some reason, there is a piano) while lamenting yet another relationship difficulty. Somehow the narrative shifts to the singer taking the role of a preacher lecturing her congregation about how to hold a man. The disjointed narrative is reflected in the strange organization of the tune and arrangement. Beginning with a piano introduction, Smith comes in with a verse of twelve bars, although it is not a blues. A very odd twenty-bar chorus follows with a patter section of sixteen bars more or less justifying the title:

I ain't here to try to save your soul—just want to teach you how to save your good jelly roll
Goin' on down the line a little further now, there's a many poor woman down
Read on down to chapter nine, women must learn how to take their time

. . . and so on.

The concluding twenty-bar chorus is chopped up in a particularly strange way: Smith sings the first four measures, Johnson solos on the following eight (referencing his own 1925 composition "Snowy Morning Blues" along the way), and Smith sings the concluding eight. The combination of biblical and sexual imagery doesn't quite jell in any narrative way, suggesting that in live performance there might have been some other explanatory parts that did not fit on the recording.

Johnson's accompaniment here is perhaps his least successful for Smith. The unusual layout of the tune and arrangement was perhaps not comfortable for him and his attempts to create supporting patterns often clash with the busy vocal line.

SWEET MISTREATER/LOCK AND KEY

In addition to being one of the first great jazz pianists, Johnson was perhaps better known during the 1920s as a composer of a wide variety of songs for the stage and for individual performers. Two of these were featured on the second session he did with Smith.

These two songs were recorded on April 1, 1927 ("Lock and Key" was immediately released on Columbia 14232-D, but "Sweet Mistreater" was held back until the following autumn—Columbia 14262-D). Both were compositions by Johnson with lyrics by Henry Creamer, who was also responsible for "Whoa Tillie, Take Your Time," discussed in chapter 3. By the late 1920s, Creamer's regular partner Turner Layton had relocated to England, and he had joined forces with Johnson to create a number of show tunes (including those for *Keep Shufflin'*) and soon-to-be standards such as "If I Could Be with You One Hour To-night."

When looked at together, these two songs demonstrate a look backward and forward in the history of popular music and Tin Pan Alley song form. "Lock and Key" is typical of a number of tunes recorded by Smith to that point. After a piano introduction, a sixteen-bar verse locates the singer as a partner dissatisfied with her man. After threatening to shoot him at the Barbers' Ball

They'll hear a shot and see you duck and when the smoke has cleared away
then the band will crawl from behind the stand and then you'll hear me say . . .

the singer goes into the thirty-two-bar chorus, which is in the older, march trio style (ABAC), stating her intention: "When I get home, I'm gonna change my lock and key / When you get home, you'll find an awful change in me," although one wonders why she would need to do that if she did her job at the Barbers' Ball well enough. Her lyrics of revenge then go into a sixteen-bar patter section that demands the return of the clothing she has given him, including his underwear, which is then followed by another chorus with different lyrics.

One can imagine the hilarity that this song might generate in an audience, especially considering Smith's well-documented violent streak and unwillingness to submit to second-class treatment from co-workers, fans, or romantic partners.

On the other hand, "Sweet Mistreater," though structured in exactly the same way, omitting the somewhat old-fashioned patter, features a thirty-two-bar AABA chorus (with some slight differences in the "A" sections). By 1930, this form had largely eclipsed the earlier march structure but both existed side by side in this particular recording session among the works by the same composers. This tune is, in fact, one of the earlier examples of this form to include what became one of the most common harmonic progressions on the "B" (or "bridge") section. The lyrics again tell the story of a wronged lover, although this time from the point of view of the man, whose high-class woman is running around with other men. For those commentators who attempt to see autobiographical reflections in Smith's songs, "Sweet Mistreater" would have to be looked at as Jack Gee's expression of his marital state at this time.

Unfortunately, these were Johnson's only recordings with Smith for the next two years, but the further results of their collaboration in 1929 represent one of high points (if not the artistic apex) of her recording career and is discussed in chapter 6.

AFTER YOU'VE GONE/MUDDY WATER

Fletcher Henderson's band had returned to the Roseland in early February 1927 after a short Midwestern tour and were busily engaged in the recording studios for the next two months or so. Fortunately, Frank Walker had booked Bessie Smith into the studio several times during that period, using Henderson and several of his musicians on two of them. The first session was done on March 2 and featured "Bessie Smith and Her Band" with Joe Smith, Henderson's new trombonist Jimmy Harrison, Bailey and Hawkins on clarinets, Henderson, and Dixon. Two of the tunes ("Alexander's Ragtime Band" and "There'll Be a Hot Time in the Old Town Tonight") have been discussed in chapter 2, but the remaining two were interesting examples of songs more associated with contemporary jazz repertoire.

"After You've Gone" was composed by Creamer and Layton in 1918, but did not find much success until it was recorded by a number of different singers and bands in 1927 and 1928. Though it came to be regarded as an up-tempo jazz number in the 1930s, it was originally a slow, blues-influenced song sung her by Smith in its original version. Her singing, accompanied by Henderson's musicians, makes a fascinating comparison with the version recorded five weeks later by Sophie Tucker accompanied by a group called Miff Mole's Little Molers, featuring the cream of the white jazz musicians of the period including Mole, Red Nichols, Jimmy Dorsey, and Eddie Lang.

Of more interest is "Muddy Water—A Mississippi Moan," a brand-new tune composed by the white songwriter Peter De Rose, the black lyricist Jo Trent, and white entertainer Harry Richman. "Bluesy" in subject matter (again focusing on flooding disasters on the Mississippi at the time), the song is very much in the Tin Pan Alley vein, although the chorus is practically through-composed, with each of the four eight-bar sections being different.

Her accompanists are not of much use here—only Joe Smith is able to do even a slight amount of improvised backup (and mainly on the verse). Harrison is limited to a few "tailgate" trombone effects that were probably even then considered out of date, while the two clarinets play a monotonous harmonized figure throughout that gives the impression of a particularly nasty case of hiccups.

The tempo is so slow that there is only room on the recording for a single pass each through the verse and chorus following a short instrumental introduction and followed by an even shorter coda. Smith is in her element, with the long note values of the melody inspiring her to use her full repertoire of melisma, pitch inflection, and shading to unify the performance in a way that would have been impossible for most other singers. Her ability to sustain notes without lessening the musicality or running out of breath mid-phrase is true musicianship on both an artistic and technical level.

The subject matter of the lyrics makes for an interesting comparison with "Backwater Blues." Although Smith's tune approaches the topic from the point of view of those affected by the flood, "Muddy Water" takes a much more detached look at the situation, beginning with an idealized picture of the Old South in the verse:

Dixie moonlight, Swanee shore headed homebound just once more, to my Mississippi delta home
Southland has that grand garden spot, although you believe or not
I hear those breeze a-whispering—come on back to me

The chorus ends with a desire to return to the afflicted area out of a sense of nostalgia: "My heart cries out for Muddy Water," a perplexing point of view that nevertheless became a good seller, perhaps on the strength of the floods being so prominent in the national news that spring.

Smith's recording was successful, but from the view of the tune itself, a more sensible version was recorded five days later by Paul Whiteman's Orchestra featuring the first solo vocal recorded by Bing Crosby. Capitalizing on the bouncy feel of the lyrics, the tempo is faster and it becomes a standard dance band number rather than a lament.

HOT SPRINGS BLUES

The session Smith recorded the next day was more successful on at least one level. Four tunes were recorded, of which the best overall is "Hot Springs Blues" (March 3, 1927, Columbia 14569-D). This date benefits from superior sound quality and balance—the Columbia engineers had conclusively solved the problems presented by the switch from acoustic to electric recording by this time. The sound of each instrument and the voice are beautifully blended and allow us to appreciate the interaction between Smith and the horn players, particularly on "Hot Springs Blues." It is regrettable that the other three tunes from this date were less adaptable to the talents of Joe Smith and Green. "Send Me to the 'Lectric Chair" is a monotonous song that even defeats Bessie Smith's attempts to move it along. "Them's Graveyard Words" begins and ends with a harmonized version of Chopin's "Funeral March" between the two brass instruments and continues through a long exposition and chorus with the expected theme of the wronged woman threating mayhem on her man. "Trombone Cholly" is a comic number between the singer and trombonist Green, which is a warmup for their better-known collaboration "Empty Bed Blues" made a year later (discussed in chapter 6). Green provides the appropriate responses suggested by the lyrics ("He wails and moans, he grunts and groans—he moans just like a cow!") and the short instrumental interlude by Joe Smith and Green provides some redemption. All three of these tunes are credited again to George Brooks, raising the pertinent question of how much of the lyrics were Henderson's and how much Smith's.

Far different is "Hot Springs Blues," credited to Bessie Smith. Not released until the fall, this tune features a complete division of labor between the two horns: Charlie Green and Joe Smith (here, with Henderson, called "Her Blue Boys"), who alternate backing the singer's choruses, joining together only at the very end. Unusually, Smith begins the song without an introduction—in fact, starting on a pickup note before Henderson joins in on the downbeat of the first measure. This introduces an immediate sense of purpose and urgency to the performance, almost implying that we are interrupting a performance that has already begun. Smith's voice is likewise urgent here, verging occasionally on shouting over the accompaniment (which was not nearly as evident on the other three sides that day). Her delivery might be characterized as angry, possibly to do with the subject matter.

By the late winter of 1927, Smith and Gee had mostly abandoned all pretense of standard domestic life. They remained married and occasionally still cohabitated, but the stories from this period recounted by Ruby Walker and Maud Smith present a picture of mutual hatred and distrust. Smith was obviously happy to engage in frequent affairs with both sexes and to embrace the most hedonistic aspects of an entertainer's life on tour, and Gee was apparently moving in the direction of serial infidelity and secrecy himself by this point. Complaining frequently of imminent nervous collapse, he would leave tours he was supposedly managing to go "hunting," a recreation that Walker surmised involved prey of his own species. At some point in early 1927 Smith sent him to recuperate at a spa in Hot Springs, Arkansas, and visited him for a short period.

The lyrics to "Hot Springs Blues" are enigmatic to say the least. The third verse

> With the steam and the sweat and the hot rooms too
> With the steam and the sweat and hot rooms too
> If that don't cure you, tell me what will it do?

seems to cast some doubt on the dependability of the treatments—perhaps Smith was venting a bit about Gee's absence or the degree of hypochondria or deception he was practicing. Though interpreting Smith's recorded lyrics as autobiographical is nearly always a questionable practice, here it seems absolutely clear that her composition and recording of "Hot Springs Blues" was, like "Backwater Blues," inspired by events in her life and should be looked at in that regard.

FOOLISH MAN BLUES/DYIN' BY THE HOUR

Tommy Ladnier (1900–1939) was a trumpet player who was raised just outside of New Orleans and began playing as boy. Moving to Chicago as a teenager, he developed a reputation as an excellent blues player who, despite not possessing a flashy technique, was considered on par with Louis Armstrong as an interpreter in the blues style. After several years of playing and recording with Lovie Austin, Jelly Roll Morton, Ma Rainey, and King Oliver, he moved to New York briefly before joining Sam Wooding's dance and show band in 1925 for an extended European trip that took him as far as the Soviet Union and Berlin. During this trip he was heavily featured as a soloist, making numerous records, and became a better reading musician. This improved technical ability allowed him to join Fletcher Henderson's band shortly after he returned to New York at the end of 1926.

Henderson, who had been looking for a trumpet soloist who could fill the void left by Armstrong's departure at the end of 1925, used Ladnier extensively as a soloist, picking up where Armstrong had left off as a blues specialist and counterweight to the refined style of Joe Smith, who was still in the band. Henderson recordings such as "Snag It" and "I'm Coming Virginia" feature each of them, emphasizing their stylistic differences, especially in regard to rhythmic approach. Ladnier remained with Henderson until the end of 1927, after which he left to tour Europe again with Wooding, remaining there until 1931, playing mainly with Noble Sissle's group.

Possessing a forthright, declamatory style mainly focused on the middle register, Ladnier used mutes more than Armstrong, though his open playing demonstrated a broad sound and power that also produced a similar sort of swing. Although his reading was never more than adequate, Ladnier managed to deal well enough with the parts in Henderson's dance band (as well as those led by Wooding and Sissle) to earn his keep, and his solo contributions were highly rated by the other musicians in the groups.

Ladnier's only recording with Bessie Smith was "Foolish Man Blues" and "Dyin' by the Hour," on October 27, 1927 (Columbia-14273-D). Along with Henderson, the accompanying group is rounded out by Henderson's tuba player, June Cole. The addition of a bass instrument provides a foundation not heard on many of Smith's recordings (not counting the film sound track, a tuba appears on only two other sessions and a string bass only on her final one in 1933), though Cole's stately two-beat contribution gives a much more old-fashioned quality to the performance. In fact, on these recordings Smith sounds considerably more like Ma Rainey than on practically any of her other sides.

The lyrics themselves were also a look back to the more theatrical strain of the Classic Blues that Smith had not been recording since her early sessions. The second title was credited to George Brooks and is mainly a collection of tongue-in-cheek blues verses:

> I'd drink carbolic acid, if it wouldn't burn me so,
> I'd drink carbolic acid, if it wouldn't burn me so,
> Then telephone the devil, that's the only place I'd go

The tempo is so slow that only four choruses are possible during the course of the three-minute recording, and the accompaniment is more taken up with novelty aspects introduced again by the Chopin "Funeral March" quote in the introduction and coda.

Far more impressive is "Foolish Man Blues," which features Ladnier at his economic best, combining the blues feeling and vocalized tone quality of Armstrong with the discretion of Joe Smith; he may have been Smith's best accompanist overall. The lyrics were apparently written by Bessie Smith, who is credited on the record. Again at such a slow tempo that only four verses could be included on the recording, "Foolish Man Blues" is in some ways a continuation of "Dyin' by the Hour," with the same themes running through the performance. The second verse introduces an unexpected trope into Smith's blues expression:

> There's two things got me puzzled, there's two things I can't understand
> There's two things got me puzzled, there's two things I can't understand
> That's a mannish actin' woman and a skippin' twistin' woman actin' man

It is unfortunate that Ladnier's year with the Henderson band occurred at a time when Smith did not record as extensively as she had in previous years and that Joe Smith was still in the picture, doing most of her sessions. It is intriguing to think how Ladnier might have spiced up some of the sessions done during the next two years when the singer's accompanists were, to put it charitably, variable.

A GOOD MAN IS HARD TO FIND

My inclusion of this song (Columbia 14250-D, September 27, 1927) in this section is more of an introduction to the next chapter, although it is an apt summation of this part of Smith's life and career. Following the session with Ladnier, Smith never again recorded with Henderson or any regular members of his band other than Charlie Green (who was in and out of the group for the rest of the decade). The Ladnier session was actually a brief curtain call for the Henderson/Smith association, with Smith's prior two sessions being made with her current touring accompanist, Porter Grainger, and some other musicians while Henderson's band was on tour in Chicago.

The song "A Good Man Is Hard to Find" was composed by the black songwriter and vaudevillian Eddie Green in 1918. Bessie Smith's 1927 recording came about because of the tune's renaissance in a show called *Vaudeville* that same year in which it was sung by Sophie Tucker. Again, the temptation is to find some kind of personal catharsis in Smith's reading of the lyrics, but she may well have been singing it since before she even knew Jack Gee, so any personal experience that might be reflected would be only in the immediate performance.

The accompaniment is by Grainger and guitarist Lincoln M. Conaway, who backed a number of blues singers from 1924 to 1927 and was apparently part of a family of string players, including Sterling Conaway and Clarence Conaway. Though not earthshaking from the point of view of interaction or innovation, they support Smith well here and on its session mate "Mean Old Bed Bug Blues." Grainger's piano is virtually inaudible, but Conaway's guitar is more prominent, especially in his triplet patterns that link the vocal lines.

Strangely, the relatively soft guitar accompaniment doesn't have the effect on Smith that it did on her April 1924 sessions (and as some of those in 1929 and 1930 would). She continues to belt out the lyrics, using the complete repertoire of shouts and growls that she employed with larger groups. Of course, intimacy of approach would not really fit with the lyrics, which are a different sort of lament:

> Lawd, a good man is hard to find, you always get another kind
> Yes, a when you think that he's your pal,
> You look and find him foolin' 'round some old gal
> Then you rave you all crave you want to see him down in his grave. . . .

These lyrics also represent some significant departures from the published lyrics. In the second chorus, she further develops those lines.

Lawd, a good man is so hard to find, we always get that roughed over kind
Just a when you think that he's your pal,
You look and find him hangin' 'round some old gal
Then you rave, child, you crave, you want to see him dead, layin' in his grave. . . .

With no other interactive accompanists, Smith had to sustain the interest by herself, and recasting lyrics was a method she probably developed onstage.

6

EMPTY BED BLUES

At some point in 1927 or 1928, Columbia either restructured Smith's contract or simply removed the guaranteed number of releases. After several years of at least twelve records (twenty-four sides) being issued annually, 1928 saw only eight, 1929 seven, 1930 four, with three in 1931 to complete her association.

Although some commentators see this as a tragic waste of talent sacrificed to the vagaries of popular taste, it was really just the inevitable shift of public opinion and the constant reinvention of popular music. Though Smith made fewer recordings after 1928, her public appearances and tours were not notably curtailed. During the next two years, she made her first appearance on Broadway and on film (both of which were unfortunately not to be repeated), as well as establishing a temporary celebrity with the upper crust of white New York society. Even if public opinion and the saturation of the Classic Blues recording market had not forced Columbia to turn its attentions to other singers, the Wall Street crash of October 24, 1929, and the ensuing Great Depression would surely have had the same effect. Even with the economic contraction of the time, Bessie Smith shows continued to tour and draw good crowds until her death in 1937.

The simple fact about recording in the pre–rock and roll era that is overlooked by most historians is that musicians (especially those active before 1940 or so) did not view the business of recording as anything more than a supplement to their main income, which was playing dance music. Even someone as successful as Bessie Smith had been during the first five years or so of her studio career did not expect to make that much money in front of the horn or microphone. The concept of artists receiving royalties and lifetime annuities from their recordings is a modern idea, and the wails of injustice about the situation would probably have seemed very strange indeed to those artists. The most desirable result of having recordings regularly issued on a strong label such as Columbia was in the publicity that those companies would provide in the press: a new Bessie Smith record would be announced well in advance of her tours, and its appearance in stores and play in private homes would be crucial to the buzz that would get people into the theaters.

The labels would of course profit from good sales, but the composers and music publishers would reap even more benefit from the publishing royalties that would be generated not only by the records themselves, but by the resultant sale of sheet music, published orchestrations, and other records related to them. Very few musicians (two exceptions being Jelly Roll Morton and Duke Ellington) thought of their records as anything but transient documents. Numerous accounts exist of both black and white musicians active in the studios in the 1920s and 1930s who, in their senior years, were bemused if not befuddled by a never-ending stream of young enthusiasts and scholars who questioned them relentlessly about the circumstances of and personnel on their early records.

One of the most significant factors in the reduction of Classic Blues on record was the rise of Country Blues. Solo male singers (almost invariably black and often with physical handicaps) were recorded, usually accompanying themselves on guitar performing their own material. Although they sang a wide variety of material including gospel, folk music, and popular numbers in person, these singers were most prized by record labels for their blues. Talent scouts such as Ralph Peer and Frank Walker traveled to sometimes remote areas of the South to find singers that they felt had something to offer on recordings and made a point to find performers with material that could be presented as original, even if they were essentially arrangements of traditional music (Evans 1982, 72–73). These singers were quite cheap to record, as they required no other accompanying musicians, and even easier to exploit, considering most of them were illiterate and basically rootless. From 1926 on, singers such as Charley Patton, Mississippi John Hurt, Papa

Charlie Jackson, Tommy Johnson, Blind Willie Johnson, and Blind Willie McTell recorded for a variety of race labels, but the most influential and prolific was Blind Lemon Jefferson.

Jefferson was a blind guitarist and singer who was born in Texas in 1893 and lived a somewhat transient existence before settling in Dallas in the 1910s. He supported himself mainly as a street performer; as such, he was expected to sing a variety of musical styles depending on the audience. He managed to develop an advanced guitar technique and came to the attention of Mayo Williams, a black talent scout for Paramount records, who brought him to Chicago in late 1925 to begin recording. Although his first releases were gospel songs under the name "Deacon L. J. Bates," Jefferson had a career recording blues for Paramount (and, briefly, OKeh) that lasted until his death in 1929 and produced around one hundred recordings of his own songs.

Jefferson began the tradition of these Country Blues singers, which continued throughout the 1930s and had the dual effect of influencing the direction of African American popular music and also of virtually eliminating the demand for recordings by the Classic Blues singers. The gradual fading of the style had been commented on and predicted as early as 1925, but by 1928 or so (long before the onset of the Great Depression, which is often given as a reason), most of the best female blues singers were essentially finished making recordings. Ma Rainey's last twenty recordings were made during 1928 and featured accompanists light-years different from the jazz musicians she had been working with for most of the rest of her career. Bessie Smith continued making records intermittently until 1931 (with one curtain call in 1933), but Columbia attempted to reinvent her as more of a popular singer, largely eschewing the country flavor they had experimented with a few times in earlier years.

LIFE

As detailed in chapter 5, Bessie Smith's domestic life was gradually unraveling by 1926 or so, although that year had started with promise. It was that year that she decided to "adopt" a child—the son of one of her chorus girls whose boyfriend had abandoned her. The six-year-old boy she rechristened Jack Gee Jr. was also known as Snooks and became a part of the tour during the spring of 1926. After finishing the tour she opted out of her usual summer tent show circuit, instead spending the time at home in Philadelphia, where she had rented houses for her three sisters and their offspring. Jack Sr. was inveigled into driving his new car (bought by Smith) to Chattanooga to bring the family back, ostensibly to care for the new member.

Smith also did not record during the summer of 1926 (unusual given the fact that she was not touring), apparently having decided to take the time off completely to settle her family and presumably also to rehearse her new *Harlem Frolics* show that began a theater tour in the fall. Ruby joined the tour at some point, bringing with her school friend Lillian Simpson, who became Smith's primary love interest while Jack was away. It was from this tour (which lasted into the spring of 1927) that some of Walker's spiciest reminiscences come, as well as some of the most violent confrontations between Smith, Gee, and assorted cast members.

The occasional presence of Snooks (although he usually remained in Philadelphia under the care of Smith's sister, Viola) did nothing to help the marriage—both Smith and Gee used him as a pawn at different times to serve their own interests, with Gee ultimately taking him away and putting him into state custody in 1930. For his part, Gee apparently began a long-term affair with singer Gertrude Saunders (who later denied it), a more modern-styled cabaret singer with finer features and lighter coloring than Smith. Nevertheless, Smith's continued popularity on the tent show and rapidly declining Theatre Owner's Booking Agents (TOBA) circuits was attested to by Sam Reevin's request to Gee to produce two different shows.

According to Albertson and Walker, Jack Gee was approached by Reevin (TOBA's booking manager) early in 1928 about mounting two shows rather than the usual one for the fall season. Gee began organizing Smith's show *Steamboat Days* as a follow-up to her highly successful *Mississippi Days* show of the previous year. Apparently without being completely honest with his wife, he held back some of the money and mounted a second show that was to feature Saunders (Albertson 2003, 178–79). A look at the existing press notices for both Smith and Saunders seems to indicate that this deception may actually have taken place a year later: Smith's 1929 show *Midnite Steppers* toured the TOBA circuit throughout the fall of 1929 and into 1930, closely fol-

lowed by its second company, known as *Whoopee Girls*, a show produced by Gee and starring Saunders, who had been with the *Blackbirds*
show until November 1928 and may have spent the earlier part of the
year on the West Coast. It also toured through Cincinnati and Columbus in early 1930, both of which cities feature prominently in Walker's
story about how Smith discovered the situation and the violent scene
that erupted when she finally caught up with Gee.

Walker and Maud Smith both recalled that the shock of discovering
Gee's betrayal on both personal and professional levels sent Bessie
Smith into a depression. The discovery completely dissolved the marriage, although it is unclear whether they ever formally divorced. Fortunately for her personal equilibrium, Smith met an old friend in Chicago,
bootlegger Richard Morgan, who became her partner in romance and
business for the rest of her life. His nephew, jazz vibraphonist and
drummer Lionel Hampton, recalled that they were virtually inseparable
throughout the 1930s, and his illicit income during the waning years of
Prohibition may have offset the reduced professional opportunities she
had. Even with the change in popular styles coupled with the national
economic hardship, Smith continued mounting tours of the South or
starring in other revues virtually every year. She also performed frequently in New York in smaller clubs and venues, although her attempts
to keep her repertoire updated were often scuttled by the popular
perception of her as an old-time blues singer (which will be seen in the
discussion of her final recording session).

Despite seeing the start of her significant domestic turmoil, the last
three years of the 1920s also provided Bessie Smith several opportunities that might have been important doors to her future. The first was
her adoption by intellectual white society as part of the Harlem Renaissance. In April 1928 while headlining *Mississippi Days* at the Lafayette
Theater, she (along with Ruby Walker and her pianist, Porter Grainger)
was invited by writer, photographer, and socialite Carl Van Vechten to a
party in his Manhattan apartment. The story of what happened that
night was recounted by several of those in attendance, but all were in
agreement that although the music Smith and Grainger provided for
the upscale crowd was enthusiastically received, the scene created by a
seriously inebriated Smith was even more memorable. Probably smarting at the pretentious atmosphere and realizing that she was being
treated as some kind of exotic creature, Smith exited the party by

knocking over the host's wife and her two companions, finally crashing to the floor in the elevator after a withering profane tirade. No more party invitations were forthcoming.

The second opportunity occurred in May 1929 and was lost due to mismanagement rather than Smith's behavior. The black composer Maceo Pinkard had been rehearsing his show *Pansy*, a college-themed show set to open on Broadway in the middle of the month. He approached Smith to come in as an added attraction (but not part of the actual cast or in any way important to the plot) to sing a few numbers. The troubled rehearsal period continued into the performances, of which there were only three before the show closed. In general, the New York critics were unanimous in panning the show as a slapdash production, though most singled Smith out for praise in her role as a walk-on singer. Unfortunately, her only offer to star on Broadway was in a show that had no business being there in the first place.

The third ultimately unrequited opportunity came as an offer to star in a short film based on the lyrics to W. C. Handy's "St. Louis Blues," featuring a full band, chorus, and comics. Although the film can be seen today as an artistic success on most levels, a variety of circumstances combined to keep it from wide release, and it remained only a tantalizing possibility of what might have been (as is discussed in chapter 7).

RECORDINGS

From the beginning of 1928 until the end of her recording career, Bessie Smith did not benefit from the accompaniment of Fletcher Henderson or any of his musicians (other than Charlie Green, who played with Henderson's band irregularly during that period). The reasons for that had much to do with the scheduling of the recording sessions, all but one or two of which occurred while the Henderson band was on tour from its regular engagement at the Roseland. In addition to the matter of scheduling, the Henderson band was in flux in 1928 and 1929 owing to several things, not least of which was the departure of its musical director, Don Redman, in the middle of 1927. In addition, Henderson himself was involved in a car accident while touring in Kentucky in the summer of 1928. For the duration of his recuperation, he essentially disbanded his group, although most of the regulars were back within a month.

Far more serious was the strife over the band's participation in the Vincent Youmans show, *Great Day*, in June 1929. Apparently Duke Ellington's Cotton Club band was originally selected to play in the pit of this show, which featured a mixed-race cast. Ellington was unable to balance the time commitment for the show with his contract at the club and backed out, making way for the Henderson band. Bolstered by the presence of Louis Armstrong (who had just returned with his band from Chicago) and a white string section, the band was poised to do great things before the conductor began replacing the black musicians. Henderson apparently did not fight for his musicians and the fiasco led to several of his longtime players leaving and the band essentially breaking up for a period. His band, though reorganizing and still touring, made no recordings until October 1930.

Many fans consider Smith's recordings from February 1928 until November 1931 to be some of the worst of her career. The majority are—with the exception of her own contributions—dire in regard to the accompaniment. Her seven recording dates (producing eighteen released tunes) from February until August of 1928 were directed by Porter Grainger, who had been her pianist on tour. The repertoire was not bad, but the musicians he selected—presumably he selected them—harkened back to the inept accompaniment of her first year's recordings. Fortunately, a few rose above the general level of mediocrity.

EMPTY BED BLUES

Ironically one of Bessie Smith's most successful recordings came years after her initial straight blues successes. "Empty Bed Blues" was a two-sided record (Columbia 141312- D) recorded on March 28, 1928, of a song by J. C. Johnson (who had a long career composing tunes in tandem with Henry Creamer, James P. Johnson, and Fats Waller, among others), featuring Charlie Green and Grainger. Green had left the Henderson band at some point in 1926, and although he occasionally rejoined it for tours or recording dates, he did not again play with it on a regular basis. He remained in demand as a blues accompanist and soloist with other bands until his death in the mid-1930s. Grainger had begun as Smith's touring accompanist in September 1927 and continued his association with her at least until the end of the summer of 1928 and her show *Mississippi Days*.

Beginning with a four-bar introduction by Green and Grainger, the first side continues with five choruses of blues loosely organized around the theme of the loss of a man who had been remarkably gifted in sexual satisfaction. After the first chorus setting the scene of waking up and not finding him in bed, the lyrics proceed to work over a catalog of sexual metaphor.

> He knows how to thrill me and he thrills me night and day [x2]
> He's got a new way of loving, almost takes my breath away

The final chorus on side one cites the reason for her loss, ending with the accusation that her girlfriend shared her man's charms: "From the way she's raving, she must have gone and tried it too."

The flip side of the record (continuing a song on another record, even a flip side, was highly unusual for popular music at the time) begins with a four-bar introduction. After a momentary disagreement between Smith and Grainger about the blues form in the first chorus (Grainger skips the middle four measures), five more choruses of similar material further extends the metaphors, particularly with kitchen references, and leaves even less to the imagination. After the final chorus, an eight-bar coda (omitting the middle four measures of the blues form as Grainger had tried to do earlier) provides the "moral" lesson referencing her faithless friend who stole her man.

Grainger provides a full-sounding accompaniment that still has a rhythmic lift not evident on the Clarence Williams sides, but it is Green's contribution that probably went a long way toward selling the record. On the first side, he growls and snarls in the most suggestive way possible in answer to her sly comments. His technique is on display much more here than on most of his other blues accompaniments; he clearly knew his instrument better on a technical level than he is usually given credit. On the second side, he plays with a straight mute, giving a more "nasty" sound but continuing in the humorous vein. When Smith sings about how her man came home one evening with his "spirit way up high," Green responds with a rising glissando that is not difficult to interpret.

Humorous interaction of this sort was apparently used by Smith in her stage show as well, although Green never appeared with her outside of the studio as far as the record indicates. Several accounts of her touring groups mention a trombonist named Joe Williams, who fortunately made a few recordings with her in August 1928, demonstrating a close stylistic affinity with Charlie Green.

ME AND MY GIN

Little is known about Williams other than that he toured with Smith (making two recording sessions with her in August 1928, presumably while Green was with Henderson on a tour of the Middle Atlantic states) and that he may have occasionally played with Henderson's band as well. His playing is earthy and aggressive in the style of Green's very elemental blues accompaniments, which may have made him an attractive and probably cheaper substitute on theater and tent show tours.

Of the two sides recorded on August 25, 1928, "Me and My Gin" (Columbia 14381-D) is perhaps slightly better than the other ("Please Help Me Get Him off My Mind," which is more traditional in content, although less suggestive than "Empty Bed Blues") and is often cited as autobiographical due to its interesting admission of alcohol dependence.

> Don't try me nobody, oh, you will never win.
> Don't try me nobody 'cause you will never win.
> I'll fight the army, navy, just me and my gin.

This song is also interesting in that it is devoid of any romantic or sexual imagery, at least until the last chorus where "I don't want no pork chop, just give me gin instead" seems for once to be a culinary rather than sexual reference.

Grainger and Williams both play well, although the rhythmic energy evident on "Empty Bed Blues" is not apparent here. At times, Williams drops out entirely, although in general his contributions are interesting and do not get in the way of Smith's singing, a talent not shared by some of Grainger's other choices of accompanists at the time.

STANDING IN THE RAIN BLUES

Fred Longshaw had been recording with Smith intermittently since beginning as her accompanist in the fall of 1924. Although Grainger had taken over in the fall of 1927, Longshaw apparently returned to replace him for two recording dates in February 1928 and possibly toured with her at this time as well. Charlie Green was involved in both sessions, and Joe Smith had apparently been contracted but had to cancel (possibly due to a Henderson tour in Baltimore and Philadelphia), necessitating the last-minute substitution of Demas Dean on cornet. Dean had been playing with several Harlem bands and was later to have a long career with Noble Sissle's band in Europe and America.

Dean left an interesting account of what recording with Smith was like (Reed 1998, 183–84). He cited Smith as the best of all blues singers, largely based on her sound and vocal quality and said that she was "relaxed" and easy to work with (surely not the prevailing opinion). He said that there was no written music other than a lead sheet for the piano and that the rehearsal was conducted in the studio and involved only a run-through of the introduction and a listen to the lyrics.

Of the five numbers Dean recorded with Smith, "Standing in the Rain Blues" (Columbia, 14338-D, February 21, 1928) is one of two blues and perhaps the best example of one of her late-period recordings that best captures the spirit of some of her earliest sides. After a standard introduction by Dean, Green, and Longshaw, Smith begins with an uncharacteristically poetic sentiment:

> Standin' in the rain and ain't a drop fell on me,
> Standin' in the rain and ain't a drop fell on me,
> My clothes is all wet, but my flesh is as dry as can be

The accompaniment is not to the level of inspiration that Smith was probably used to, but it is competent. Longshaw's playing is highly inventive; his ascending runs behind her lament "Rain, rain, rain, don't rain on me all day" in the last chorus are effective in a way that the horns really are not on this recording. Green seems disinterested and often off mic, while Dean is rhythmically stilted, although tasteful in his fills at the end of Smith's lines (the cornet and trombone alternate lines throughout all the blues on these sessions).

WASTED LIFE BLUES

From May 1929, most of Smith's recording sessions seem to have been organized by Clarence Williams, who was not shy about advancing tunes that he had either written or published and were heavily geared toward the novelty vaudeville songs that Smith had been singing in her shows for a decade or more. Although some were reasonable, many were highly repetitious and dependent on not-very-subtle sexual double entendres that were probably inspired by the success of "Empty Bed Blues" in March 1928. During that time was one short period of light: the three sessions she recorded in August and October 1929 accompanied by only James P. Johnson.

I cannot agree with either Brooks or Schuller that Johnson was ultimately an unsatisfactory accompanist for Smith because of his prodigious technique and the fact that he was not reluctant to use it. Similar criticisms have been made of the sides with Louis Armstrong for the same reason but with more justification. On the sessions with Johnson her singing has a flexibility and drive as well as a soulful quality that only occurs on certain other recordings and rarely in the complete combination heard on these sessions. The material covered during these sessions is also far more varied, ranging from basic blues to fairly sophisticated pop tunes, showing off Smith's versatility and general musicianship. The conclusion is inescapable that his guidance (both at the keyboard and presumably as music director behind the scenes) brought out elements of Smith's artistry (and professionalism) that both had been and would remain hidden by average material and indifferent accompanists.

The whole question of what songs and how much of them Smith composed is a difficult problem. "Wasted Life Blues" (Columbia 14476-D, October 1, 1929) was originally credited to Jack Gee; the lead sheet submitted to the Library of Congress lists him as the sole composer, but his name is crossed out and "Bessie Smith" is written underneath. It is generally accepted on the admittedly biased testimony of Walker and Maud Smith that Gee was basically illiterate so the idea of him writing a song is unlikely. A number of Smith's recordings were attributed to Gee (including "Cold in Hand Blues" and "Reckless Blues," on each of which he is credited as co-composer with Fred Longshaw), leading to the conclusion that she signed certain numbers over to him, perhaps to buy him off. The stamp on the copyright submission says that it was received on November 29, 1929, almost two months after the song was recorded and presumably a month or so after it was released. By this point, Gee and Smith were not on good terms, so why she would have gifted him with a composer credit (potentially leading to income) is an interesting question. If one believes Walker's claims of deviousness and deceit on the part of Gee, it is not difficult to consider that he might have submitted the copyright on his own.

One piece of evidence supporting this is that the lead sheet is wrong in several respects. First, one verse is missing from the copy. Second, the refrain "Oh me, oh my wonder what will the end be, oh me, oh my, wonder what will become of poor me" is transcribed incorrectly. Smith sings the first syllable as a pickup, whereas the lead sheet has it as the first beat of the measure. The handwriting is also shaky and not at all neat or professional, suggesting that James P. Johnson did not write it out. Smith's accompanists were apparently usually responsible for creating the transcription to submit for copyright, as the number of attributions to "George Brooks" (aka Fletcher Henderson) demonstrates.

The song itself is completely unlike anything else Smith is generally credited to have written. With virtually no elements that could be considered African American, theatrical, or even popular in the 1920s style, "Wasted Life Blues" is more of a folk song of the sort that might have been influenced by "Heart Songs" or even Victorian parlor ballads of the nineteenth century. For his part, Johnson contributes to this feel by aping a polite, tremolo-heavy style on both the introduction and his short solo, as well as occasionally behind the vocal.

The lyrics are likewise very different from Smith's other efforts. The sorrowful, self-pitying lyrics are in tone much different than her other blues songs that, whether narrative or pastiches of stock phrases, are rarely hopeless and often triumphant. The final verse

I've traveled and wandered almost everywhere to get a little joy from life
Still I've gained nothing but wars [possibly "worries"] and despair, still struggling in this world of strife

employs a tone and vocabulary very much at odds with any other song she recorded. Smith's singing is also restrained and controlled until the end where she ascends to a confidently struck high C, climaxing her lament and rounding off what is a beautiful, if completely uncharacteristic, performance.

DIRTY NO-GOODER'S BLUES

The flip side of "Wasted Life Blues" was "Dirty No-Gooder's Blues" (Columbia 14476-D, October 1, 1929), another tune credited to Smith. This time, there is no problem believing that this is her own work:

> There's nineteen men livin' in my neighborhood
> There's nineteen men livin' in my neighborhood
> Eighteen of them are fools and the one ain't no doggone good

Singing of the eternal romantic struggle of conflict between the sexes, Smith here employs a tempo much faster than she did on similar blues earlier in her career, showing that tastes in musical performance had changed significantly over the course of the decade.

Employing occasional growls and snarls, Smith imparts an intensity to the performance that combines with Johnson's rolling accompaniment to produce a performance that is perhaps not as powerful as some of her early recordings but that still succeeds as a duet between equals. On the final chorus, she reverts to the earlier blues practice often associated with Ma Rainey using only "Lawd" or some variation of it on the first two lines, answering it with "That dirty no-good man treats me just like I'm a dog." Where Rainey might have hummed (as Smith had done occasionally on records), the employment of an actual word intensifies the mood of loss and its subsequent confusion beautifully.

BLUE SPIRIT BLUES

"Blue Spirit Blues" (Columbia 14527-D, October 11, 1929) is another highly unusual tune. A minor blues, the song was composed by Spencer Williams, and in Gunther Schuller's words represents "fire and brimstone visions worthy of a Hieronymous Bosch" (Schuller 1968, 241). Unlike some of her earlier minor and minor-inflected blues ("Haunted House Blues," "Sing-Sing Prison Blues," for example), "Blue Spirit" is not played for laughs, emphasizing African American stereotypes like fear of the dark and evil spirits. Called by Edward Brooks "an obsessive

Gothic twilight" (Brooks 1982, 162), the lyrics are again unlike anything else Smith recorded or, for that matter, that Williams wrote. Conjuring up a demonic underworld as it appeared in a dream, the words represent an expressive sophistication far beyond anything Smith had been called on to declaim on records or possibly in person.

> Demons with the eyelids dripping blood [x2]
> Dragging sinners to that brimstone flood

Johnson's accompaniment begins and ends with the typical silent movie cliché found on many Smith recordings but in between spins a continuous series of inventive phrases and backgrounds that in a couple of places threatens to go off the rails. Smith demonstrates her confidence and musical stature by refusing to be led, and Johnson returns in each case. Her delivery is not her usual booming declamation but instead a restrained recitation that highlights the threatening feel of the lyrics.

DON'T CRY BABY

This song, the last of the series with Johnson as her sole accompanist, is perhaps the most modern and complex tune Smith ever recorded. "Don't Cry Baby" (Columbia 14487-D, October 11, 1929) was a Tin Pan Alley tune by Johnson with Saul Bernie and Stella Unger (two composers active on Broadway in the 1920s and not known for any other successful tunes). Smith's recording was the only one made at the time the tune was composed, but it enjoyed considerable success in the early 1940s on the strength of popular recordings by Erskine Hawkins, Lucky Millinder, and Count Basie.

Consisting of a verse and thirty-two bar AABA chorus in the up-to-date style, "Don't Cry Baby" demonstrates a musical logic not always in evidence on Tin Pan Alley fare of the time. The sixteen-bar verse (also in AABA form) employs a chromatic descending line that begins on the highest note of the song, an unusual musical gesture that makes life difficult for the singer. Unlike the slower, swing era recordings of the tune, Smith's version of "Don't Cry Baby" is taken at a loping tempo that gives time for two passes through the chorus, enabling Smith to employ some tonal variation while Johnson creates a more active background on the second chorus.

The lyrics certainly give lie to those attempting to see autobiographic meaning in all Smith's songs from this period. The ameliorative words of the verse

Honey, please don't cry, listen to me there's no reason why we shouldn't agree
If I hurt your feeling, I apologize you're the only one that I idolize

really could not be further from what we know of Bessie Smith's romantic temperament or dealings with her husband at the time. The chorus likewise sounds an apologetic note on the bridge: "Won't you forgive, won't you forget. . . . Just start new" seems to represent a very different character from the blues singer of her early records.

This tune (and its session mate "You Don't Understand" by Johnson, Spencer Williams, and Clarence Williams) represents the musical direction that Smith was beginning to take. By the mid-1930s trade and personal accounts recall her singing sophisticated pop material such as "Stardust" and "Smoke Gets in Your Eyes," which were sadly never recorded. It should come as no surprise that she continuously updated her repertoire; as a popular entertainer she had to please the public, which then as now is a constantly renewable entity. By 1930 she had been singing professionally for twenty years and the songs that were popular at the beginning of her career were long past their shelf life.

KITCHEN MAN

"Kitchen Man" was composed by Andy Razaf (who presumably wrote the clever lyrics), Maceo Pinkard, and Alex Belledna. Pinkard and Belledna were responsible for the music and book, respectively, of the Broadway disaster *Pansy* mentioned earlier in this chapter. Running for two performances in the middle of May 1929, *Pansy* produced no songs that have survived in memory, with even Smith's feature "If the Blues Don't Get You" never being recorded. How she came to record "Kitchen Man" (Columbia 14435-D, May 8, 1929) a week before the opening is a mystery, given that the song is not listed in the playbill for the show. Perhaps it was used as an encore and was anticipated to be a success; it is difficult to believe that she was brought in to sing only one tune.

It is not only the tune that is interesting about this session, but the accompaniment. Beginning with this session, Clarence Williams returned as Smith's regular accompanist and studio recording director (he was involved in eight of her last thirteen sessions from this point until her last Columbia session in 1931). For this date he brought the pioneering white guitarist Eddie Lang. Lang was a regular in the recording studios throughout the 1920s with his usual partner, violinist Joe Venuti, as well as a blues accompanist (sometimes going by the name Blind Willie Dunn), and duo with Lonnie Johnson. Here, Williams is mercifully in the background while Lang is given prominence in the accompaniment role. His lacy single note playing in the introduction could be by no one else, and his appropriate and supportive answering lines to the Smith's lyrics create an intimate atmosphere that belies the sense of the lyrics.

The other two tunes from this session ("You've Got to Give Me Some" and "I'm Wild about That Thing") were both by Spencer Williams and were in fact the same basic melody in the same key. Very lightweight novelties of the sort that many vaudeville singers were doing at that time, they highlight the much more sophisticated "Kitchen Man," which was a catalog of culinary metaphors for sexual performance. Setting the scene at an upscale house where Sam, the cook, has just quit, the verse leads into the chorus, where the mistress of the house is lamenting his departure. A thirty-two bar AABA form, the chorus lists many of Sam's finer attributes, with the bridge and last eight measures of the second chorus reaching a climactic moment of sorrow for the bereft lady:

When I eat his doughnuts, all I leave is the hole
Any time he wants to, why, he can use my sugar bowl
Oh, his baloney's really worth a try, never fails to satisfy—I can't do without my kitchen man

This sort of bawdy suggestive lyric was becoming common by the late 1920s in records aimed at African American audiences; Ethel Waters recorded Razaf's "My Handy Man" ("He threads my needle, creams my wheat, heats my heater, chops my meat") three months after Smith's "Kitchen Man." The final recording of Smith's Columbia contract was "Need a Little Sugar in My Bowl," which continues with "I need a little hot dog in my roll," giving an idea of the perception of audience interest. Even more earthy expressions of sexual prowess could be found in contemporary songs like "Tight Like That," "Shake

That Thing," and "Four or Five Times," showing the direction that popular music was taking in general.

NOBODY KNOWS WHEN YOU'RE DOWN AND OUT

For the sessions run by Clarence Williams during this period, he was the sole accompanist on only two of them. For the most part he used musicians who were active with him in the studios at the time. Williams did not have a regular performing band per se, but he was perhaps the most active African American musician in the studios, leading several hundred sessions up to the mid-1930s and featuring many of the top jazz players of the day. By the late 1920s he had settled into a routine of recording mostly his own tunes or those published by his company with a small stock company of musicians including cornetist Ed Allen and drummer/washboard player Floyd Casey, both of whom appear on several later Bessie Smith sessions.

On the day following the close of her Broadway debut, *Pansy*, Smith recorded what became an anthem of the Depression in general and the popular perception of Smith's career in particular—"Nobody Knows You When You're Down and Out" (Columbia 14451-D, May 15, 1929).

Once I lived the life of a millionaire, spendin' my money, I didn't care
I carried my friends out for a good time, buying bootleg liquor, champagne and wine
Then I began to fall so low I didn't have a friend and no place to go
So if I ever get my hand on a dollar again I'm gonna hold on to it till them eagles grin

Composed by Jimmie Cox in 1923, this tune was originally a cautionary tale for people whose fortunes were good during good times but that changed meaning completely following the stock market crash in October 1929 (one month after Smith's recording was released).

Introduced by a sonorous tuba line supporting two saxophones playing long-held notes and the gentle, almost tentative sound of Allen's cornet, "Nobody Knows When You're Down and Out" promises something a bit more understated than the usual Bessie Smith recording. Ed Allen (1897–1974) was born in Nashville but raised in St. Louis, where he became one of the lineage of accomplished trumpet players from that city. Although known for his quietly authoritative playing on Clar-

ence Williams recordings, he was presumably an accomplished technical musician as he played in pit bands and big bands throughout the
1920s and 1930s in Chicago and New York.

Smith's singing is anything but tentative, signaling a defiance in the
face of fortune's reversals. After her first verse and chorus, Allen plays
an eight-bar solo with a plunger mute that could not be further from
the style of either Armstrong or even Joe Smith in its deferential tone
suggesting emotional vulnerability. This moment of tender exposure is
followed by Smith, this time in a more reflective mood, as she trades
one- and two-bar phrases with herself, first humming, then singing.

NEW ORLEANS HOP SCOP BLUES

"New Orleans Hop Scop Blues" (Columbia 14516-D, March 27, 1930)
was a tune by the black blues pianist and composer George Thomas
(whose sister was blues singer Sippie Wallace) and published by Clarence Williams. Unusually for a blues recorded by a singer during the
1920s, this song was conceived as more of an instrumental, and its lyrics
make no attempt to be dramatic or to tell a story, but instead to present
the steps for a dance. Such songs have a long tradition in American
popular music, "Ballin the Jack" and "Shake, Rattle and Roll" being two
other examples. After a verse citing the dance as a native New Orleans
creation (where even "the white folks do it too"), the chorus uses the
blues form to instruct the listener in the steps:

> Glide! Slide! Prance! Dance!
> Hop! Stop! Take it easy, honey!
> I can never get tired of dancin' those Hop Scop Blues

For this session, Williams brought a full front line with him: trumpeter Louis Bacon (a Chicago native who was a newcomer to New York
making his first recording), Charlie Green, and clarinetist Garvin Bushell (a veteran of the Harlem dance band scene whose career went
back before 1920). Although the lyrics are clearly not profound, the
accompaniment was designed to be up to date, with Green and Bacon
soloing. Smith herself sings with a powerful swing that makes one wonder what she would have sounded like a decade later in front of a big
band. Though the horns acquit themselves admirably (particularly Ba-

con, whose style was definitely a look toward the swing era), the rhythm is leaden, with Williams's plodding accompaniment effectively sapping any rhythmic energy the horns and Smith attempt to infuse into what might have been a rollicking performance but for the presence of a bass or some other rhythm instrument.

BLACK MOUNTAIN BLUES

"Black Mountain Blues" (Columbia 14554-D, July 22, 1930) is an interesting combination of the more theatrical strain of late 1920s blues, country elements, and standard Classic Blues. Composed by J. C. Johnson, the song is a succession of blues choruses making liberal use of hyperbole that Smith sings with obvious relish.

> Back in Black Mountain, a child will smack your face
> Back in Black Mountain, a child will smack your face
> Babies cryin' for liquor, and all the birds sing bass

The accompaniment here is unusual. During this period when Clarence Williams's presence was felt in most of her sessions, here the pianist is the otherwise completely unknown Steve Stevens with Ed Allen. Allen's playing is much more forthright here than it was on "Nobody Knows When You're Down and Out" or many of the dozens of tunes he recorded with Williams. His sound is more prominent and his muted responses to Smith's lines are tasteful while still occasionally flashing some technique. By the end of the song she is inspired to reach to another high C near the top of her range on the word "devil," showing that her technical abilities were still intact at this late stage in her recording career.

LAST SESSION

Bessie Smith's contract with Columbia was not renewed after her November 20, 1931, session was completed. Her trips to the recording studio had been less frequent since 1927 due to a combination of new styles taking the place of what she did so well and the Depression severely contracting the recording industry. She was to make a final studio appearance on November 24, 1933, for OKeh records (since

1926 a subsidiary of Columbia, usually releasing its lower priced records) at the behest of John Hammond.

Hammond (1910–1987) was an offspring of the fabulously wealthy Vanderbilt family and had rebelled against his conservative upbringing by embracing African American music, particularly blues and jazz, while in prep school and college. Although some black artists and commentators (Ruby Walker in particular) were highly suspicious of his motives and saw him as an opportunist, the overall body of his contribution to American popular music is remarkable. During his career as a record producer spanning fifty years, he was directly responsible for signing artists as diverse as Billie Holiday, Benny Goodman (later to be Hammond's brother-in-law), Count Basie, Aretha Franklin, Stevie Ray Vaughan, Pete Seeger, and Bob Dylan to record contracts.

Hammond had been exposed to Smith and the Classic Blues singers while in high school and as a recent Yale dropout was intrigued with the idea of bringing some of them back into the studio with up-to-date jazz musicians. His original intention of having Smith sing some of her old blues hits or at least tunes in that style was overruled by the singer who felt that newer, more theatrical tunes would be better. This was a decision he regretted in hindsight, although it demonstrates the power and influence Smith still had and how she presumably had been allowed to make some of the repertoire decisions earlier in her recording career as well. The four tunes were all credited to "Wilson," either one or both of the husband-and-wife team known as Grant and Wilson. Pianist and singer "Kid Socks" Wilson and his wife Leola Wilson (also known as Coot Grant) had been touring the black vaudeville circuit since the early 1920s and were prolific songwriters, with as many as four hundred tunes to their credit. Though the songs recorded that day were certainly not the "sophisticated" type Smith was known to be singing at that point in her career, they are certainly more modern sounding than much of her repertoire had been for the final year or two of her Columbia contract.

A large part of the modern sound of these recordings is due to the band, which was overall the best group Smith had appeared with in a studio. The pianist on the date, Buck Washington, was a well-known entertainer on the black vaudeville circuit with his partner, John "Bubbles" Sublett, and was chosen by both Louis Armstrong and Coleman Hawkins to make duo recordings at different times. Guitarist Bobby

Johnson was a busy Harlem musician who had played long periods with Charlie Johnson's Paradise Orchestra in the 1920s and Chick Webb's band in the 1930s; he was also active in the studios, recording with Red Norvo, Taft Jordan, and Benny Morton, among others. Billy Taylor Sr. (whose son and namesake became a well-known jazz pianist and educator) had a tremendously long and successful career that stretched from playing with Jelly Roll Morton and McKinney's Cotton Pickers in the 1920s through long 1930s stints with Fats Waller and Duke Ellington and finally to freelancing in New York into the 1970s. Although Smith's notorious distrust of drummers kept them from this date (there had been drums on only two of her Columbia sessions and the film), the piano, guitar, and bass rhythm section provides a more solid support for her than any other with which she had recorded.

The front line of the group was basically an all-star cast for the day. Trumpeter Frankie Newton was one of the best of the swing-era stylists on his instrument and can be heard on hundreds of small group recordings during the 1930s and 1940s, as well as in bands led by Teddy Hill, John Kirby, and Lucky Millinder. Chu Berry was a young tenor sax player who was, at the time, a devotee of Coleman Hawkins but whose style was in the process of maturing. He ultimately took Hawkins's place in the Henderson band of the late 1930s and was featured in the groups of Teddy Hill, Benny Carter, and Cab Calloway. Hammond, being known for his attention to social justice issues and the cause of integration, tried to make his recording dates during the 1930s mixed wherever possible, but his inclusion of the white trombonist Jack Teagarden was more than just a nod to political correctness. Considered the foremost trombonist in jazz by the late 1920s, Teagarden was playing at the time in the Paul Whiteman Orchestra, which gave him little outlet for improvisation, so his occasional recording dates outside Whiteman's purview usually found him in an inspired mood. As an added bonus, clarinetist Benny Goodman (who was just about to form his famous big band, launching the popular period of the swing era) stopped by after recording with another band in the same building to contribute a few notes to "Gimme a Pigfoot and a Bottle of Beer."

DO YOUR DUTY

"Do Your Duty" (OKeh 8945) is in some ways a throwback to Smith's earlier blues songs in which she restricted her range in favor of a shouting delivery. Her initial entrance (after the traditional four-bar introduction) sounds more like Sophie Tucker than Bessie Smith, although that impression is quickly dispelled by her repertoire of bent notes and wailing delivery. Although in the modern thirty-two-bar AABA form, this song is cast more in the older style, even featuring the stop-time feature on the "A" sections of the last chorus.

The lyrics are definitely a throwback; generally a story familiar to fans of Smith's records, "Do Your Duty" presents the picture of the singer lamenting her inattentive boyfriend, though spiced with a degree of retribution informed by frustration.

> If you make your own bed hard that's the way it lies
> I'm tired of sleepin' by myself but you're too dumb to realize

Smith's voice is perhaps a bit thicker than it was during the previous decade but retains its power and natural swing along with a suppleness that perhaps comes from the fact that she is no longer responsible for controlling the rhythmic pulse.

What casts this as something well beyond Smith's previous recordings is the lightly swinging rhythm that begins in the introduction and carries the piece through to the end. An entire chorus between the vocal parts is divided in eight-measure segments between Newton, Washington, Berry (taking the bridge, which is based on the bridge to George Gershwin's "I Got Rhythm," itself a modern touch), and Teagarden. Each of these four short solos demonstrates a modern concept of rhythm and harmony (with the possible exception of Washington's—he was at best a marginal pianist), with Berry's double-timed contribution and break standing out.

GIMME A PIGFOOT AND A BOTTLE OF BEER

Of the four Wilson tunes recorded on this session, "Gimme a Pigfoot" (OKeh 8949) is the most "retro" in terms of structure. After a piano intro calling to mind any number of similar efforts by Clarence Williams and Fletcher Henderson, Smith enters with a spoken interlude over a vamp that then leads to the verse, which the singer slows down considerably.

Up in Harlem every Saturday night when the highbrows get together it's just too tight
They all congregate at an all night strut and what they do is tut, tut, tut
Old Hannah Brown from cross town gets full of corn and starts breaking 'em down

From here comes the sixteen-bar chorus in the older style, which celebrates the joys of a backcountry Prohibition speakeasy in which a piano player plays a central role. There follows another chorus of improvisation in a very modern swing style by Newton, who demonstrates significant technique as well as advanced ideas. The final vocal chorus is essentially the same lyrics as the first, although Smith varies a few of the phrases, most notably the last half, where she substitutes "reefer" for "pigfoot." Marijuana was not technically illegal in New York until the mid-1930s, and its use was widespread in entertainment circles, so the reference was not merely an inside joke.

Smith's voice again displays a somewhat thicker quality, but it is significant that her range extends to a high E flat (twice), which she had used only rarely in previous recordings. This certainly proves that her voice was not failing her at this point; on the contrary, her phrasing and native swing were at their peak on this final session. It is fortunate that this peak coincided with one of her most successful recording sessions backed by what was probably the finest overall group she worked with.

7

ST. LOUIS BLUES

Experiments connecting sound to the moving picture had been ongoing practically since the beginning of the film industry. A variety of roadblocks prevented any sustained attempt to commercialize sound film before the end of the 1920s, some technical, some financial, and some artistic. Lee DeForest patented a system of putting sound on film that he called Photofilm in 1921. Some early experiments with that system (including a film of the popular African American vaudeville duo Sissle and Blake) were well received, but the coolness of the larger movie studios due to the cost of changing to the new system effectively ended the experiment.

By 1926, Warner Brothers had begun to use its Vitaphone system to create a method of using phonograph records in conjunction with films. Several popular films including *Don Juan* (1926) and *The Jazz Singer* (1927) were released with sound tracks (in the former case, just music, and in the latter, a combination of music and dialogue). More important from a historical perspective were the numerous short subjects that were released with them.

Initially, these one-reel films featured musical acts—opera singers, orchestras, and musical novelty acts that were playing in New York (where filming was done) at the time. When these shorts proved as popular as the features, Warner Brothers began looking further afield and filmed popular music acts, including a number featuring black bands. Claude Hopkins, Don Redman, and Cab Calloway were just a few of the entertainers who were filmed by Vitaphone in the late 1920s and early 1930s, although for the most part their films were just presentations of one or more of their hit songs—precursors to latter-day music videos.

Other companies began developing their own systems as well and it soon became clear that sound film was not merely a novelty. African American actors and musicians were not frequently featured in these early films, although some (including Ethel Waters, Mamie Smith, and Victoria Spivey) were given brief solo turns in larger films, much as if they had been walk-on acts in a Broadway revue. When the white director Dudley Murphy proposed making a series of short (two-reel) films based on African American popular music and featuring black actors and musicians, it was a fairly radical proposal. Fortunately he was allowed to go ahead with the plan, assisted by a brain trust of black stage veterans and writers, with the engagement of Bessie Smith and the cooperation of W. C. Handy being the most important elements. The decision to use a particular song as the narrative for each of the three films (the other two were "Black and Tan Fantasy" for the 1929 Duke Ellington film of the same name and "Frankie and Johnny" for the Gilda Gray film *He Was Her Man* of 1931) was also unusual, suggesting an operatic component to the projects.

"ST. LOUIS BLUES"—THE SONG

W. C. Handy (1873–1958) had a long and distinguished career in music (see chapter 1). Known as the father of the blues, Handy was responsible for some of the most enduring compositions in that repertoire, but none more popular that "St. Louis Blues." Published in 1914, the tune became an almost immediate sensation and was recorded numerous times by the end of the decade, although almost all the recordings were made by white performers. Consisting of two distinct blues strains (the first beginning "I hate to see the evening sun go down" and the second "Got the St. Louis Blues, just as blue as I can be") separated by a sixteen-bar bridge with a tango beat ("St. Louis woman, with her diamond rings"), the tune is well constructed and thematically varied.

Tom Lord's Jazz Discography lists more than 2,100 recordings of the song, which does not take into account concert, country, and ethnic versions, which probably would double that total. The fact that so many different artists were inspired by "St. Louis Blues" shows the timelessness of the music and the fact that it has come to be regarded as a kind of American folk tune, joining other published songs such as Foster's "Old Folks at Home" and "Yankee Doodle" as classic expressions of the American spirit. Handy's tune is remarkable in that it was a true crossover hit, composed by an African American composing in a vernacular black style.

Most of the early recordings of "St. Louis Blues" were by bands, with only a few vocal treatments, of which white singer Marion Harris's 1920 version for Columbia was the most popular (she recorded it again in 1923 for Brunswick). Sung in a precise manner with only token blues inflection, Harris's first version was a virtual reading of the sheet music with orchestral accompaniment, probably the same way she was doing the song in vaudeville. Slightly more bluesy was the 1921 OKeh recording by the black New Orleans singer Esther Bigeou, although it still inclines toward a more glib, novelty stage version with little to recommend it in the way of depth of feeling.

The first truly great recording of the song was done by Bessie Smith (Columbia 14064-D, January 14, 1925). As the first tune of a long session ("Reckless Blues" is discussed in chapter 4), "St. Louis Blues" also represents the first meeting between Smith and Louis Armstrong, both of whom had probably been playing the tune for the better part of a decade at that point. With only the quaint sound of Fred Longshaw's harmonium to provide harmonic and very limited rhythmic support, the interplay between the cornet and the voice is foregrounded. For the first time in the recorded history of the tune (and one of the first times in recorded history period), a song by a black composer is performed by an all-black group in a deep and thoughtful way. This recording can be heard as a spiritual (albeit one using secular lyrics), summoning a degree of emotion and impassioned playing virtually unknown on recordings to that point.

Smith follows the AABC structure of the tune (as did Harris and Bigeou) but adds nothing beyond an introduction of only one note—no solos, no coda, no theatrics of any kind. Indeed, the incredibly slow tempo would not allow for any extras considering the duration of a ten-inch record of the time. The focus is entirely on the lyrics as declaimed by Smith and the instrumental responses of Armstrong. Smith did not play for white audiences very often during this period, but it is not a stretch to believe that she would not have played a tune with the depth of emotion like this one for them.

ST. LOUIS BLUES—THE FILM

Bessie Smith's two recorded performances of "St. Louis Blues" bookend a significant falloff in the popularity of the genre. Just as the canaries gave way to the more traditional blues singers, so they began to give way to the Country Blues singers: Blind Lemon Jefferson, Big Bill Broonzy, and the like. Though Bessie Smith's popularity was great enough to keep her working steadily through the Depression, her opportunities to record became less frequent by the late 1920s. One moment of Indian summer came with the appearance of sound movies and the inevitable rush to employ musical acts.

St. Louis Blues was filmed over the course of several days in June 1929 in the RCA Photophone studio in Gramercy Park, Manhattan. Director Dudley Murphy had been active in directing and producing avant-garde films in France in the mid-1920s, including making important contributions to Fernand Leger's *Ballet Mechanique* of 1924, which was made in conjunction with George Antheil's composition of the same name. Murphy had experimented with making films to preexistent scores, in effect realizing or inventing programmatic elements. His *Soul of the Cypress* using Debussy's "Prelude to the Afternoon of a Faun" was one of several "visual symphonies" he made for Universal in California in 1920 and is considered to be one of the first avant-garde films made in America.

Murphy, a white upper-class native of Massachusetts, had briefly attended MIT before serving in the Air Corps in World War I. After returning to the United States in late 1924, he resumed working in the film industry in New York, directing Gloria Swanson and others during his period of apprenticeship. This period coincided with his growing interest in African American music, which had begun in France when he was introduced to some of the expatriate American musicians and entertainers performing in Paris. In New York he became acquainted with Carl Van Vechten, Marc Connolly, and other members of white society and intellectual circles who were similarly inspired by the music and art of the "Harlem Renaissance" and who frequented Harlem nightlife. In this way Murphy developed a familiarity with some of the musical figures of the scene, including Bessie Smith and Duke Ellington.

In 1929, Murphy proposed making a series of films based on African American music. In his autobiography, W. C. Handy claims that the inspiration to make *St. Louis Blues* was his—that he coauthored a screenplay with Kenneth W. Adams based on the song and submitted it to RCA. Whichever came first, the screenplay was accepted and Murphy hired to direct. At some point it was suggested that Bessie Smith be considered for the starring role—she was scheduled to be in New York that month for her Broadway debut in *Pansy*, which had closed after a week in early May 1929. The filming and recording was done in late June and the completed film was released on September 8 of that year.

According to Handy, a choral version of "St. Louis Blues" included in Lew Leslie's show *Blackbirds of 1928* antedated the film and may have convinced him of the marketability of a concert treatment of his most popular blues (Handy 1969, 224). Presumably at his recommendation some of the most familiar names in the black New York music establishment were engaged. The orchestra, directed by pianist and composer James P. Johnson (discussed in chapter 6) consisted of the top black musicians of the day, many of whom had played for the recently disbanded Fletcher Henderson Orchestra. The voices were from the famous Hall Johnson Choir, which was to become a fixture in films depicting African American life for the next twenty years. The choral arrangement was by Handy and J. Rosamund Johnson, a legendary figure even then with a career as a musician, actor, and composer stretching back to the beginning of the century. No mention is made of the identity of the instrumental arranger, but presumably the two Johnsons collaborated. The actors in the film were all longtime participants in the black vaudeville scene in New York and several were familiar faces in early sound films as well.

THE MUSICIANS

Composer Vincent Youmans was known for a string of Broadway hits since the early 1920s, including the big hit of 1925, *No, No, Nanette*. Seeing the unprecedented success of Jerome Kern's *Showboat* in 1927,

Youmans determined to make his next show a salute to the Old South, complete with a mixed-race cast and, going Kern one better, a black pit band. He apparently approached Duke Ellington via his manager Irving Mills to use his Cotton Club Orchestra as the core of the orchestra but scheduling and contractual issues scuttled Ellington's participation. Youmans then engaged Henderson, who canceled his usual summer tour of New England to join in rehearsals in Philadelphia following the close of his season at Roseland at the end of April.

In order to augment Henderson's usual twelve-piece band, Youmans added a string section and possibly a few other horns, including Louis Armstrong, who was specially brought in from Chicago. Unfortunately, the producers determined that Henderson was not up to conducting a Broadway show and he was replaced, as were about half of his musicians (including Armstrong). The choice to replace them with white musicians was a major point of contention in the black press at the time and caused a great deal of bad blood between some of the dismissed musicians and Henderson, whom they felt did not defend them. The show itself was not a success, lasting only a few dozen performances before closing altogether.

The breakup of the Henderson band freed up several musicians who were then hired by James P. Johnson to fill out his band in the film, though not as many as has sometimes been suggested. Alto saxophonist Arville Harris and drummer Kaiser Marshall were both members of the group that was involved with *Great Day*, and Marshall was later vocal about his disappointment in Henderson, for whom he never worked again. The trumpet section can be identified both aurally and visually as Joe Smith and Sidney DeParis; Smith had left the Henderson band at some point at the end of 1928 and was freelancing around New York, while DeParis was featured with Charlie Johnson's band. Smith's broad tone is recognizable in the film itself, but especially during the musical portion of the opening credits, where DeParis's unique plunger-muted style is also prominent. Both trumpeters (as well as Marshall) recorded with McKinney's Cotton Pickers later that fall before going with other groups. The trombonist is likely Charlie Green, although he is only on camera for a few seconds. The saxophone section is probably Harris on alto and Happy Caldwell on tenor (identifiable by comparison with contemporary photographs). Identifying the third saxophonist (who also plays the clarinet solo in the fast portion) is more problematic; I believe it is Cecil Scott, who had played with Henderson occasionally in the middle 1920s and who at the time was leading his own band. The guitarist is probably Bernard Addison (he is also the only musician heard during the first reel of the film) and the bass (not tuba) player is Harry Hull; both Addison and Hull played with Johnson later in the year. Contrary to the assertion of Chris Albertson, there is no string section in the band.

Francis Hall Johnson (1888–1970) was born in Georgia and exposed to classical music as a boy. After a long apprenticeship playing violin and viola in black orchestras in New York, he began concentrating on choral music, especially choral settings of classic African American spirituals. He founded the Hall Johnson Choir in 1925 and toured and concertized with it extensively through the 1950s. In addition to formal concerts, the choir was well represented on films during its career, the most notable of which was *Green Pastures* of 1936. Director Dudley Murphy was obviously partial to the group, including it in two of his three 1929 films, *St. Louis Blues* and *Black and Tan* (the latter featuring Duke Ellington's Cotton Club Orchestra).

J. Rosamund Johnson (1873–1954) was, with his brother James Weldon Johnson, a significant figure in African American literary and artistic circles. After musical training at the New England Conservatory, Rosamund began composing songs (the best known of which was the so-called Negro national anthem—"Lift Every Voice and Sing" in 1900) and writing shows for black entertainers in the first two decades of the twentieth century. He was also actively engaged in theatrical productions through the 1930s. He contributed at least part of the script to *St. Louis Blues*, presumably the dialogue in the first reel.

THE CAST

The cast of *St. Louis Blues* is drawn from the ranks of black Broadway and vaudeville performers. Dancer Jimmy Mordecai (who plays Jimmy the Pimp) was part of the celebrated trio Wells, Mordecai, and Taylor, who were considered among the top dance acts of the era. In addition to his work here, Mordecai also appeared in the starring role of James P. Johnson's *Yamekraw* of 1930 and supported Paul Robeson in *Emperor Jones* (also directed by Murphy) in 1933. Jimmy's younger girlfriend is played by Isabel Washington, who, with her sister Fredi (who is featured in Murphy's subsequent 1929 film *Black and Tan* with Duke Ellington), had worked for W. C. Handy's music publishing company in the early 1920s and became a chorus girl at the Cotton Club. She gave up the stage shortly after this film to marry Adam Clayton Powell Jr.

The supporting players include Alec Lovejoy as the janitor, a busy film and Broadway performer in all-black productions. Edgar Connor is the short gambler; he and Lovejoy were teamed as piano movers in *Black and Tan* and as comic menials in *He Was Her Man* (1931—the third film of the trilogy, featuring singer and dancer Gilda Grey). Composer and blues entrepreneur Perry Bradford makes an appearance as the craps player who informs the others that Jimmy is with his paramour "in Bessie's room." The audience at the club consists of members of the Hall Johnson Choir and the waiters were apparently imported from a Harlem club.

The film itself is a two-reel short subject designed to be shown in conjunction with a feature. Initially paired with the popular *Bulldog Drummond, St. Louis Blues* opened in New York to generally positive reviews, although some reviewers were made uneasy by the fairly graphic portrayal of lower-class existence. As the film opens, a dice game is going on behind the staircase of what turns out to be a rooming house. An intervention by a janitor is ended by bribing him to keep his mouth shout, after which Jimmy the Pimp appears. He, aided by the inspiration of a pretty woman, soon wins all the money, and the game breaks up as they go into one of the rooms. It turns out that the room is the one Jimmy shares with Bessie, his other girlfriend who apparently keeps him. When she finds the two lovers, a fight ensues during which Bessie evicts both her rival and the janitor who comes to inquire about the noise. Her demeanor turns softer with Jimmy, whom she begs to take her back. Jimmy pushes her to the ground and leaves as she begins to sing the opening lines of "St. Louis Blues."

The action in the second reel shifts to a cabaret where a pan shot shows the faces of the audience and the band, which has begun to pick up the tune. Bessie is shown at the bar in a state of despondency as she continues singing the song. After singing the whole form (including the minor strain) over the laments of the choir and background parts of the band, she stops. The band then plays a fanfare and goes into a fast version of the tune, encouraging the audience and waiters to dance. As they continue the scene, Jimmy appears at the door and is greeted warmly by everyone except the oblivious Bessie. After doing a solo dance, he goes to her and his body language suggests reconciliation. She joins him in a slow dance that ends with him again pushing her to the ground and taking the money she has in her garter. A quote from *Rhapsody in Blue* ends the piece as Bessie again takes her place at the bar and the chorus sings the final verse and chorus of the tune.

Dudley Murphy apparently insisted that the music be recorded live, rather than the usual process of prerecording the sound track and then fitting the action to the sounds. Although the overall sound quality suffers somewhat (there probably was only one overhead microphone used), the live sound contributes to the realism of the scene, especially in terms of preserving what Bessie Smith may actually have sounded like in person. Her stage presence in the musical segment is extraordinary and the sheer power of her voice is evident when riding over a ten-piece band and large chorus. Her acting in the scenes with Jimmy is, to say the least, stilted. Murphy later recalled her as being uneasy in front of the camera—this in contrast to Mordecai, who projects ease in every word and action.

After *St. Louis Blues* was released, it had a short period of success (and positive reviews) in the New York area. It received little press or distribution outside of the vicinity for a variety of reasons. Its grittiness was probably not destined to appeal to audiences beyond urban areas, and in areas with large African American communities, the technology in theaters may not at that point have allowed for sound films. Some of the African American establishment also objected to the depiction of what they considered an embarrassing element of black society. Of course, the fact that the initial release of the film came less than two months before the stock market crash was perhaps the biggest reason that *St. Louis Blues* disappeared quickly and for many years was thought to be a lost film.

The craps game and room scenes are probably what caused the outcry from the NAACP when the film came out. The concern that this seamier side of African American life should not be celebrated on film caused a degree of alarm among the black press, which promoted this, one of the first sound films with an all-black cast, remarkably little. The unabashed sensuality and violence of the scenes bothered some who felt that such images of African American life needed to be suppressed or at least not acknowledged. Years later when the film was rediscovered, liberal groups voiced concern not over the reality of the depiction, but about its presentation of stereotypical black characters. Most of the characters in the first reel are variations of stock characters from African American theatrical presentations of the era.

A "BLACK" FILM

The question of what defines a "black" film is an open-ended one—there seems to be no agreed-upon standard in scholarly literature. Usually, some combination of an all-black cast, black writers, directors, and producers creating films aimed at a black audience is cited, but perhaps the most useful working definition is Allen Woll's, that black theater be "by, about, with, for and related to blacks, but need not include every one of those attributes." (Douglas Turner Ward, quoted in Woll, 1989, xiii). Continuing with Woll, it is important to note that in film (as in theater) "it has been difficult to establish historical continuity since the creation, evolution, and shape of the black musical has changed so abruptly and so often since the turn of the century."

Though a few early films (notably the silent films of Oscar Micheaux) were virtually free of any white enterprise, the movie industry from the middle 1920s on has been controlled by large corporations involved in financing, production, and distribution. Virtually no films made during that period could be considered to be completely outside the white mainstream. *St. Louis Blues* probably comes as close as any, with an entirely black cast and production team (save for the director, who had an apparently sincere appreciation for and interest in African American culture). Nevertheless, it was underwritten and released by Sack Amusement Company, a small Texas-based distributor that financed black films from the 1920s until the late 1940s and used the technical services of RCA Photophone and its studio in Gramercy Park. Although RCA Photophone was owned by the new RKO company (incorporated under the control of RCA in October 1928, with its first release being *Syncopation* at the end of March 1929), *St. Louis Blues* was apparently not released by the larger company, which presumably wasn't interested in race films.

CHARACTERS

The history of all-black theatrical productions reaches back to the late 1800s when African American performers began to claim a portion of the minstrel phenomena. Originally an all-white lampooning of black ethnicity, the classic minstrel show began to feature black entertainers lampooning the lampooners, as it were. The vogue for all-black shows (for both black and white audiences) took off by the 1890s with African American actors and musicians traveling with circuses, tent shows, and even producing Broadway shows. Will Marion Cook and Bob Cole produced *Clorindy, or the Origin of the Cake Walk* in 1898. This was quickly followed by various revues and sketch shows featuring Bert Williams and George Walker, among other actors who had been touring the black vaudeville circuit since the early 1890s.

The characterizations that grew out of this varied yet focused professional sphere (many performers had active and even simultaneous careers in all the above entertainment modes) were recognizable comic archetypes overlaid with ethnic stereotypes. Donald Bogle identified the principal figures as they were represented on film as "Toms," "coons," "mulattoes," "mammies," and "bucks." Other scholars such as Lisa Anderson, Robert C. Toll, and Thomas Cripps refined these definitions to reflect their own work, but the fundamental flaw in applying them to *St. Louis Blues* is that the evidence each cites comes from films in which the black characters played in support of whites. Much of Bogle's typology is created from *Birth of a Nation*, the 1915 D. W. Griffith epic about the Reconstruction period in which most of the African American roles were played by whites in blackface (Bogle 1996, 3–18). Though its director was white, *St. Louis Blues* was an otherwise all-black production, and its characters demonstrate numerous examples of boundary bending in terms of stereotypes.

The representation of women in early film is a rich topic beyond the scope of this discussion but suffice to say that stereotypical feminine characterization held sway for the most part. In the case of the representation of African American women, the dual concerns of gender and racial stereotyping were at work, although the Bessie Smith character in *St. Louis Blues* presents a much more complex figure than the norm in 1920s film.

In many of the narrative forms in which she appears, the figure of the ethnic woman is located (even if in apparently minor ways) outside of dominant American cultural values. What this may have meant for female filmgoers was the opportunity to engage and identify with a figure uniquely privileged to defy the social order of white, patriarchal capitalism. (Negra 2001, 11)

The character played by Bessie Smith in *St. Louis Blues* is definitely "located outside of dominant American cultural values" in Diane Negra's terms. Though some feminist writers have lamented her ultimately unsuccessful attempts to deal with the dominant gender paradigms in her romantic life, the Bessie character represents a figure of power not often seen in female (especially African American) film roles of the time. Although she is not able to assert her emotional independence from Jimmy, she nevertheless has economic power over him—she pays for his room, clothes, and the trappings of his masculinity. Physically, she also asserts her dominance over her domestic rival, the janitor of the apartment building (representing authority) and, in an abstract sense, the musicians and chorus, whose performance is entirely sublimated to hers in terms of intensity, volume, and concentration.

Following Bogle, Lisa Anderson identifies three types of black female character on film: the "mammy," the "tragic mulatta," and the "jezebel" (Anderson 1997, 2–6). The mammy is large, happy, and sexual, whereas the tragic mulatta is sad and ultimately flawed due to the presence of white ancestry. The jezebel is, simply put, a slut who is "dangerous because she appears capable of undermining the patriarchal notions of family" (Anderson 1997, 88). Bessie exemplifies elements of all three without being more of any one than the others. She physically resembles the mammy and the qualities of ferocity and independence mentioned by Bogle while obviously embodying the sorrow and flaws of the mulatta, presumably without the white bloodline. Finally, the jezebel is represented by her physical and financial dominance in the romantic relationship that clearly undermines any notion of the traditional family.

The other female role in the film is the otherwise unnamed "pretty yaller woman" played by Isabel Washington. Her action is contained in the first reel, and she functions as the more traditional "vamp" character who is Jimmy's mistress (after Bessie). More clearly in the jezebel tradition than Bessie, Washington's character is likewise dangerous but

only to Bessie and her ideas of the domestic norm. Bogle presents no
such type, but suggests that his "tragic mulatto" includes elements of
the jezebel.

The most entertaining character is Jimmy. A "buck," Jimmy drives
the action, being the only character who holds influence over Bessie.
Although corresponding to Bogle's description of the type as oversexed,
savage, and violent (Bogle 1996, 13), Jimmy also maintains an urbanity
and degree of class that is not evident in the standard typology. Mordecai's portrayal is nuanced and beautifully balanced—clearly the best
acting in the film is by him, although some of his voice is lost to the
single microphone in his scenes during the craps game and in the bed-
room.

Alec Lovejoy has a short but effectively comic role as the janitor in
the first reel. While representing some of the more noble characteris-
tics of the "Tom" ("hearty" and "submissive"), he is also like the "coon,"
shiftless and conniving, a trickster figure in his surface attempt to fulfill
his job as an employee of "that white man" though quickly accepting a
bribe to look the other way and allow the craps game to continue.
Nevertheless, when his authority is threatened—in this case by the
brawl between the female characters—he attempts to assert himself
and to use his position by threatening eviction, his reward being a
beating administered by an irate Bessie. By being both a stereotype of a
lazy and ultimately ineffective black worker, as well as a trickster who
subtly exerts control over his white employer, Lovejoy's janitor undermines the standard stereotypes.

Thomas Cripps refers to "two codes" of discourse presented by black
actors during the pre–World War II period:

> one created by writers and producers for mainly white audiences, the
> other sent by black actors to their "hep" and mainly black audiences
> for whom it provided a satiric and sometimes unconscious backbeat
> to the main line of the movie. (Cripps 1990, 35)

These codes are roughly analogous both to the idea of signifying in their
intentional subversion of the norm and to the filmic concept of diagetic
and non-diagetic. The first code can be seen as diagetic in that it is part
of the surface representation of the film, whereas the other is non-
diagetic in that it is part of an underlying current meant to be represen-

tational or used (in Cripps's words) as "an external social appendage to it."

Cripps was also one of the few to make critical comments about the film. He aptly sums up the variety of characterizations by saying that "in every instance old stereotypes took on new dimensions" (Cripps 1990, 206). Bogle also discusses African American actors and actresses who fought against the stereotypical categorization he derived, but his examples (Sammy Davis Jr., Sidney Poitier, Richard Pryor, Whoopi Goldberg, among others) all did their work at least two decades after *St. Louis Blues*. This film and other examples of all-black productions from the silent and early sound era are ripe for assessment under these parameters, perhaps in comparison with how the first black minstrel shows used the conventions of the style to turn the idea of racial ridicule on those who initiated it.

RECEPTION OF THE FILM

> The cinema had, from its very beginnings, been steadily rising in the social scale, and the middle classes are far more decorous and squeamish about the seamy side of life than the lower classes; the Hays Code (1933) marks middle-class dominance (Durgnat 1969, 117).

The issue of film censorship is practically as old as film itself, but the middle 1920s represented its first wave of central organization with the reign of Will Hays beginning at the behest of the Hollywood studios to restore public confidence in the wake of the Fatty Arbuckle and William Desmond Taylor scandals. By the last years of the decade the censors had been rendered largely ineffective due to the overwhelming number of films being produced and their own lack of authority over the studios. It was not until 1933 that the Hayes office was given the power to enforce the 1930 Motion Picture Production Code, requiring that all films released after July 1934 receive a certificate of approval. In light of the new, post-1930 code, *St. Louis Blues* would have raised red flags with its representation of brutality, seduction, marriage (i.e., the lack of), and possibly sympathy for criminals (Jimmy), although its presentation of the seamy side of poor African American society would likely have been deemed its worst offense.

Following the short heyday of black musical film in the late 1920s and early 1930s, the Hayes Code, coupled with the standard racism in the entertainment industry, severely limited the roles for African American actors and musicians. With the exception of a handful of films made by black filmmakers, Hollywood restricted blacks to servile, usually comic roles that were almost exclusively nonthreatening and performance oriented.

8

INFLUENCE

In September 1937, Bessie Smith was traveling with the *Broadway Rastus* show through the South. A far cry from the shows she had led ten years earlier, with their slick chorus lines, opulent costumes, and sophisticated musical accompaniment, this one was more like an early tent show in which Smith was the headliner but not the star. In the early morning hours of September 27 she and Richard Morgan were driving on Highway 61 toward their next destination in Darling, Mississippi, when the car Morgan was driving collided with a mail truck. The force was concentrated on the passenger side of the car where Smith was sleeping and resulted in critical injuries. A passing car containing two doctors stopped to help, although their car was demolished by a third vehicle before they could take Smith to the hospital. After a while an ambulance came and took her to the local black hospital (not to the white hospital where she was refused admittance, as the legend had it), but the severity of her injuries was well beyond the means of medical help.

Bessie Smith was taken back to Philadelphia and her funeral about a week later was remembered as one of the largest in the city's history, giving lie to the claim that she had been forgotten by the time she died. In the eighty years since her death, Smith has been credited as an influence by dozens of singers, many of whom have recorded tunes that she either wrote or popularized and in several cases have dedicated entire albums to her repertoire and style. Smith was also the subject of one of the first full-scale rereleases of earlier recordings on long-playing records. In 1951 producer George Avakian issued four LPs each of Bessie Smith and Louis Armstrong recordings on Columbia, following the 1950 success of his three-LP survey of Bix Beiderbecke's career. These albums remained in the Columbia catalog until they were superseded by the first complete issue of Smith's recordings on five double-LP sets in 1971, produced by John Hammond. These in turn were superseded by Chris Albertson's five double-CD volumes in 1991, which also included many alternate takes and one disc of edited audio reminiscences by Ruby Walker.

What made Bessie Smith stand out from her contemporaries to such a degree that she remains a focal point in American popular music history since she began recording? This is a difficult question to answer after almost a century of listening to her records, although one that can be asked about Louis Armstrong as well. Though each of these two artists clearly brought something new and even revolutionary to the table, we have become complacent in our listening and naturally assume not that they were especially groundbreaking, but that their contemporaries were somehow inferior. The contributions made by Armstrong on records in the 1920s are obvious when listened to side by side with those of other trumpet players from the same period. The influence that he exerted over both older and younger players is inarguable. In the opinion of Buster Bailey, who recorded frequently with both performers, "Bessie was the Louis Armstrong of the blues singers. She had more original ideas for blues and things than the others did" (Shapiro and Hentoff 1955, 246). With Bessie Smith, the comparison with her contemporaries is perhaps not as stark, but her long and varied recording history presents a singer leaps and bounds ahead of the average popular singer of the 1920s.

First, Smith's concept of rhythm was, like Armstrong's, far ahead of the rest of her contemporaries. The two of them shared (with Sidney Bechet, Earl Hines, and very few others in the middle 1920s) a feeling for the beat that in musical terms veers toward compound rather than simple meter. Simply put, they felt the division of the beat into three parts, while most other jazz and dance band musicians of the time felt it divided in two. This rhythmic disagreement creates some of the most interesting conflicts on their records; see, for example, Smith's early and late recordings featuring older-styled dance band players who were clearly not up to the challenge of playing with her. Armstrong's recordings with the Henderson band are likewise stark in the differences between the playing of the band (which consisted of the most accomplished black players in the idiom at the time) and his solos, which completely transform the rhythmic feel. Smith's rhythmic authority is likewise on display on any number of records in which she unilaterally controls the tempo, sometimes forcing all her accompanists quickly to change courses in midstream.

Second, Smith's voice was simply a fantastic instrument. Capable of an incredibly wide dynamic range, it was focused and full in every register, with an unerring sense of pitch that was to some degree dictated by that centered sound and her own superb ear. By the last year or two of her Columbia contract, she was also doing more *singing* as opposed to the shouting that many blues singers affected. Although her earliest blues recordings (and, sadly her very last ones) often displayed a limited range (a result of the songs themselves rather than the singer), she recorded enough sides (see especially the James P. Johnson accompaniments of 1929) to begin to step beyond her comfort zone. By the later period in her recorded career, she was singing more musically and taking on more challenging material than anyone of her generation other than Ethel Waters and perhaps Alberta Hunter—this at an age when many singers began to display a deterioration in vocal quality and contraction in repertoire.

Last but not least, Smith had an incredible stage presence. In an oft-repeated quote, New Orleans guitar player Danny Barker compared the experience of seeing her live with a kind of "mass hypnotism" that he attributed in part to the influence of Pentecostal church practice (Shapiro and Hentoff 1955, 243). Her participation in the *St. Louis Blues* film discussed in the last chapter gives at least a taste of this stage presence as well as the breadth of sound she produced.

INFLUENCES AND LEGACY

Bessie Smith's influence extended decades and hundreds of performers acknowledged her as a model in one way or another. Some, such as Ruby Walker, Mildred Bailey, Connee Boswell, and Bob Wills acknowledged her directly, referencing her actual performances. Others, such as Mahalia Jackson, Billie Holiday, and Janis Joplin were acquainted with her primarily through recordings and found in her voice a connection to their individual situation. Later performers like Joplin and Nina Simone also found in Smith a model of a strong woman who ultimately was able to triumph over the notoriously sexist entertainment industry and who sought to replicate her success and, sadly in the case of Joplin, also replicated her personal failures. Singers of the next generation such as Big Joe Turner and Jimmy Rushing took elements of the blunt, forceful style for which she was noted and developed it into way of dealing with the different demands of the swing era, as did Ella Fitzgerald in a very different way.

Classic Blues Style

Ruby Walker

Ruby Walker (1903–1977) changed her name to Ruby Smith following Bessie Smith's death and recorded a number of sides under that name. Her contribution to our knowledge of Smith's professional and private life during the late 1920s has been discussed, although one point that should be emphasized is that she saw herself as primarily a performer who sang and danced in a number of shows and also attempted to sell herself as a singer on a few occasions, incurring the ire of the notoriously jealous Smith.

"Backwater Blues" (Vocalion 4903, March 9, 1939) was Ruby Smith's tribute to Bessie Smith two years after her death. On this session she was accompanied by James P. Johnson, featuring trumpeter Henry "Red" Allen, trombonist J. C. Higginbotham, and drummer Sid Catlett (all from Louis Armstrong's Orchestra), saxophonist Gene Sedric, guitarist Al Casey, and bass player Johnny Williams (the last three with Fats Waller's band at the time). Johnson creates some backgrounds similar to his contributions on the original recording of the tune, but the larger band inspires a different feel. Unfortunately, Ruby Smith is simply not much of a singer—her voice has nothing of the presence or intensity (let alone pitch control or interpretive power) of her mentor. She sings basically the same lyrics, although her reliance on growls and her inability to sustain notes gives an unintentionally comic feel to the performance, which is sadly at odds both with the topic of the song and the superior accompaniment.

Mildred Bailey

Mildred Bailey (1907–1951) was one of the first popular singers to cross over from the blues to identify as a jazz singer. Born in Seattle, she was part Native American (on her mother's side) and white and began listening to jazz records as well as singing professionally as a teenager. After a period with Paul Whiteman's band from 1929 to 1933, she was the vocalist with the band led by her husband, xylophonist and vibraphonist Red Norvo from 1936 to 1939 and then with Benny Goodman occasionally before doing freelance radio work in the 1940s.

Bailey was known as a flexible and highly musical singer able to handle a variety of complex material and arrangements. She had a knack for varying melodic lines as a jazz player would and a particular affinity for blues, despite her deceptively light voice. She was both a fan and a friend of Bessie Smith in the early 1930s and even performed occasionally with her at parties, a highly unusual occurrence for the suspicious Smith. In addition to her regular recordings with Whiteman, Norvo, and Goodman during the 1930s, Bailey also did a number of studio dates on which she was supported by some of the finest jazz musicians of the day, both black and white.

"Downhearted Blues" (Decca 18109) was recorded by Mildred Bailey and Her Alley Cats on December 6, 1935. The band consisted of trumpeter Bunny Berigan, alto saxophonist Johnny Hodges, pianist Teddy Wilson, and bassist Grachan Moncur. The absence of a drummer is not felt—the rest of the band is in perfect sync rhythmically, and the performance shows what Bessie Smith might have done in the studio had she been given more opportunities. Although Bailey vocally sounds nothing like Smith, her approach is quite similar: the rhythmic assurance with which she sings and her ability to bend notes and vary a line without losing the sense of the melody are familiar. Hodges is very much in the background on this record, but Berigan's sumptuous accompaniment was apparently something he also provided to Smith during a jam session on 52nd Street around the same time. Wilson was one of the greatest of the swing piano players and particularly valued as a vocal accompanist. Here he shows both abilities.

Dinah Washington

Dinah Washington (1924–1963) was born Nora Lee Jones in Alabama and was at different times in her professional life a blues, rhythm and blues, and jazz singer, and she finished her career doing albums of pop music. After moving to Chicago as a girl, Washington became active in church music, singing with a gospel choir and occasionally playing piano. This gospel influence is clearly heard in her later singing; she had in common with Bessie Smith an understanding not only of gospel phrasing, but of the stage presence that gospel singers brought to religious services. Following a few years singing in local jazz and blues clubs, she was "discovered" by Lionel Hampton, who had her sing with his band from 1943 to 1946, making her first records in the process. In 1946 she was signed to a solo contract by Mercury Records, which tried many marketing strategies to get her career going. She recorded with big bands, small jazz groups, rhythm trios, string groups, vocal groups, and full orchestras, singing a range of material from standard blues and country western songs to sophisticated pop ballads. Her first theme album, *Dinah Sings Fats Waller*, was recorded in October 1957, followed two months later by *Dinah Sings Bessie Smith*.

The only reason I include Washington among "Classic Blues" influences is that Alberta Hunter, when asked to compare singers of her day to those in the 1950s, said that Washington was the only one who was really a "blues singer" (Shapiro and Hentoff 1955, 247). What she apparently meant was that Dinah Washington embodied all the elements of the blues queens of the 1920s: the voice, the stage presence, the penchant for outlandish costumes and wigs, and probably the difficult temperament that went with it all. More than that, Washington also brought the musical integrity and background that allowed her to hold a stage by herself regardless of her accompanists.

The number of Dinah Washington's songs that might be considered to represent a legacy of Bessie Smith and the Classic Blues is staggering, so perhaps taking one from her *Bessie Smith Songbook* is the most logical. On "Me and My Gin" (EmArcy MG 36130, January 7, 1958), Washington sings in a lean style on a stripped-down song to informal accompaniment. An eight-piece group led by her husband, tenor saxophonist Eddie Chamblee, gives a bouncy backing (including a strange drum part using mainly woodblocks and rims, a technique that would have sounded corny in the 1920s). The singer triumphs over it the same way Smith did so many times during her recording career; by the last two choruses she begins to energize the band with her shouts, and the climax has an almost religious fervor when she sings

> Lord, I don't want no clothes and I don't need no bed to lay my head
> I don't want no clothes, don't even need no bed
> Don't even want no pork chops, Lawd, just give me gin instead

Washington and Smith shared a love for alcohol and each experienced numerous problems that went with it. This shared dependence as well as a mutual background in church music and many varied theatrical experiences surely informed both of their performances.

Jazz Singers

Connee Boswell

Connee Boswell (1907–1976) was one of three sisters who grew up in New Orleans and, as children, began singing together as the Boswell Sisters. Beginning instrumental study early, they were influenced by hearing African American singers who appeared at the Lyric Theater, probably including Bessie Smith, who appeared there many times. Connee (who had changed her name from "Connie" early in her career) was generally the lead singer, and she also had a successful solo career, overcoming a childhood bout of polio that left her in a wheelchair for the rest of her life. Her singing of popular standards throughout the 1930s and 1940s was a significant if underappreciated influence on black singers of that generation including Billie Holiday and Ella Fitzgerald (who singled out Boswell regularly when asked about her early influences).

The Boswell Sisters was a remarkable group that did their own arrangements and initially provided their own accompaniment. During a time when middle-class women were not encouraged to become performers, they carved a successful career in New York and Hollywood after leaving New Orleans in 1928. From their first recordings in 1925, they demonstrated an understanding of African American performance practice that was unprecedented, and this, coupled with a high degree of musicianship reflected in their complex (and relentlessly jazzy) arrangements, made them a favorite of musicians, although extensive public success eluded them.

Their recording of "St. Louis Blues" (Brunswick 7467, May 28, 1935) was part of a long run of sides that they made as a group from 1930 to 1936 for OKeh, Brunswick, and (briefly) Decca before Martha and Helvetia decided to disband the act to get married, leaving Connee to continue as a solo. "St. Louis Blues" presents the trio in a classic arrangement of their own device using sudden tempo changes, harmonic shifts, rhythmic abstractions of the tune, and improvised-sounding backgrounds. Connee begins singing responses to the melody in the second chorus and then solos on the verse, where she duets with trombone and guitar lines, showing her blues feeling before the tempo doubles in the final choruses, interspersed with her "Oh, babe" ejaculations. The final chorus and coda are a swing-era update of a final "shout" chorus, bringing the performance to an exciting conclusion.

Although Boswell mentioned Mamie Smith specifically as an influence, her own blues singing was in many ways more compelling and more deeply invested in the tradition. It is not difficult to hear Bessie Smith's influence in her singing, as well as her influence as a woman performer willing and able to take on the responsibilities of a male-dominated business.

Billie Holiday

Billie Holiday (1915–1959) was born to an unwed mother and survived a deeply traumatic childhood in Baltimore and New York that included several stays in a reform school and time as a prostitute. By the time she was fifteen, she had been exposed to jazz recordings as well as some live performances and adopted Bessie Smith and Louis Armstrong as role models for her budding singing career. She began singing in Harlem clubs around 1931, eventually catching the attention of John Hammond, who arranged for her first recording date. This date took place three days after Smith's final recording and on the same day the band (led by Benny Goodman and including Jack Teagarden) also recorded three songs with Ethel Waters, creating a fascinating overlap of traditions.

Holiday's voice was, like Mildred Bailey's, small and required the amplification that was beginning to appear by the early 1930s. This allowed for a level of intimacy that was not part of Bessie Smith's normal musical expression, although the depth of emotion Holiday could produce even on banal tunes and the rhythmic surety that informed all her recordings were clearly something she had in common with the older singer. During the course of her more than twenty-five-year recording career, Holiday recorded a number of tunes associated with Smith, including "St. Louis Blues," "'Tain't Nobody's Biz-ness If I Do," and "Do Your Duty." It was in her relatively infrequent recordings of blues that both the similarities and the differences in the two singers' approaches are most clear.

Holiday recorded her own blues "Fine and Mellow" (Commodore 526, April 20, 1939) at the same session as her recording of "Strange Fruit," a setting of Abraham Meeropol's (aka Lewis Allen) stark anti-lynching poem that became a signature tune for her. Due to the reluctance of her regular recording company (Columbia) to record the controversial song, she temporarily switched allegiance to the small jazz-oriented label Commodore. For this session she was accompanied by a working band, Frankie Newton's Café Society Orchestra, featuring the trumpeter from Bessie Smith's final session as well as a number of Harlem swing musicians (the pianist was Sonny White, Holiday's current accompanist and boyfriend).

Lyrically, "Fine and Mellow" follows the pattern of any number of Smith's tunes. Beginning with a lament about her man who "don't love me—he treats me awful mean"—the words then introduce a more contemporary flair concerning fashion at least.

> He wears high draped pants, stripes are really yellow
> He wears high draped pants, stripes are really yellow
> But when he starts in to love me he's so fine and mellow

Holiday's singing is, as was said, more intimate than Smith's, but her phrasing is no less declamatory, although it features a more melodic approach with longer lines and held notes. Whereas Smith used a florid, melismatic approach utilizing growls on some notes, Holiday tended to maintain one pitch, although coloring it with bends and scoops much slower in execution, heightening the world-weary quality for which she was known. This refinement was not reflective of a repudiation of the blues, but of an acknowledgment of the dominant swing style at the time. Holiday was a favorite of jazz musicians of the day who regarded her as an equal, another similarity to Smith and the heyday of the Classic Blues era.

Ella Fitzgerald

Ella Fitzgerald (1917–1996) was not known as a blues singer; in fact, during most of the time she spent singing with Chick Webb's band and then leading it herself after his death (1935–1942), she was regarded as an above-average pop singer with a predilection for novelty tunes. After a childhood that resembled Holiday's in some ways, she began singing with Webb and making recordings with him that quickly became the selling point of the band. By the middle 1940s she had gone out on her own and begun to absorb some of the new bebop style, often performing with the main authors of that music and adapting her own approach to feature more scat singing and improvising. Her Songbook albums in the 1950s and 1960s became best-sellers and cemented her reputation as one of the finest interpreters of the Great American Songbook as well as one of the best jazz singers of all time.

Although Fitzgerald apparently never directly acknowledged Bessie Smith as an influence, as a girl she did apparently listen to recordings by other blues singers (including Mamie Smith) and was profoundly impressed with the white singer Connee Boswell (discussed earlier). Fitzgerald was more influenced by Smith in her ability to handle the business aspect of music, including fronting and running the Chick Webb band following the bandleader's death in 1939. Musically, she returned to Smith's example in the retrospective *These Are the Blues* album of 1963.

Fitzgerald had an interesting arrangement with Verve records whereby she recorded her good-selling Songbooks in between more jazz-related releases with all-star groups as well as her touring group. It is a combination of the last two that backs her on *These Are the Blues*. Roy Eldridge was one of the foremost swing stylists on trumpet but was touring with the singer at the time, as was drummer Gus Johnson. In addition to them were Wild Bill Davis on organ, Herb Ellis on guitar, and Ray Brown (Fitzgerald's ex-husband) on bass. "Jailhouse Blues" (Verve V-4062, *These Are the Blues*, October 28, 1963) is one of the Bessie Smith tunes she included on the album—an unusual choice of material.

Beginning with an unconvincing re-creation of Smith's introductory comments on the original record, Fitzgerald sings the first chorus over sustained organ chords suggesting the sides Smith made with Armstrong and Fred Longshaw. Eldridge joins in at the end of the second chorus, adding to the impression that this was an attempt to recapture the atmosphere of those earlier recordings that had by 1963 been elevated to canonic status.

Fitzgerald's singing is far more "bluesy" than her usual approach to popular material and shows the knowledge of the style pioneered by Smith and her contemporaries, even if the influence was not direct. Following the trumpet solo, she interpolates two verses that both bring out the poetic aspects of the style in the first case and recover some of its most traditional sentiments in the second:

> When a blues first got on me they poured like a shower of rain
> When a blues first got on me they poured like a shower of rain
> And I cried all night honey, ain't that a shame?

> Going up to the country and I can't take you
> Going up to the country and I can't take you
> Nothing more that a monkey man can do

Fitzgerald's melismatic approach on these last two choruses comes as close as anything else in her career to Smith's style and vocal variations, although her execution of it comes across as more self-consciously intentional and less visceral, reflecting the sensibility of her own time.

Popular Styles and Later Blues

Mahalia Jackson

Mahalia Jackson (1911–1972) was another product of New Orleans, although she refused to perform anything but religious music for the entirety of her career. Raised in extreme poverty, she heard both recordings of and stories about the Classic Blues singers who passed through New Orleans on a regular basis. She was not tempted to answer the siren's call of popular music at the time, but she always admitted loving the sound of Bessie Smith's voice and what she did to color the pitch and personalize songs.

Jackson moved to Chicago in 1927 and became actively involved in the gospel scene there, including traveling as a song demonstrator for composer Thomas A. Dorsey. After a few unsuccessful recordings in the 1930s, she began recording a string of hits in 1947, first for Apollo and then for Columbia. She also transitioned into a concert artist, appearing at Carnegie Hall, the Newport Jazz Festival, and venues around the world.

It was at the 1958 Newport Jazz Festival that she recorded a stunning version of "He's Got the Whole World in His Hands" (Philips 429.583BE, July 6, 1958) that, with secular lyrics, could be a spectacular blues performance. Her second phrase, "He's got the whole world, right in his hands," utilizes a blue note that was not an especially important part of gospel music (at least until then). The short stop-time section midway through the performance bears interesting comparison with Smith's many recorded examples using the device; the rhythmic security shared by both performers contributes to their stature and ability to dominate any performance. The deadly slow tempo (accompanied by only piano, organ, and bass) completely foregrounds her voice, and the majestic quality of it is impossible to overlook. A comparison with Bessie Smith's performance in the musical portion of *St. Louis Blues* shows incredible similarities in vocal sound, style, and artistic focus, making the "queen of gospel" perhaps the most direct descendant of the "empress of the blues."

Jimmy Rushing

One of the finest singers of the big band era was Jimmy Rushing (1901–1972). Born in Oklahoma, he became active in the Kansas City jazz scene of the 1920s, first as a pianist (he had significant musical training), and then as a singer, specializing in blues. After periods singing and recording with Walter Page's Blue Devil Orchestra and Bennie Moten's band, Rushing became a charter member of Count Basie's band, singing with it from 1935 until 1951 and being a significant part of its popular success. Following the initial breakup of that group he went out on his own, touring solo and making dozens of albums until shortly before his death.

By the middle 1930s, black big bands (especially those from the western territories) frequently featured blues singers. Rushing was a particularly valuable commodity in that he could sing other things as well as read music. Many of his early recordings with Basie were blues that were taken from common stock material (some of which can also be heard on Smith's records), but he gradually began to be featured on pop songs and more sophisticated blues, such as "Harvard Blues" (OKeh 6564, November 17, 1941).

"Harvard Blues" is an unusual song based on a poem by Boston newspaper columnist and jazz writer George Frazier recounting in cryptic fashion numerous elements of the Harvard undergraduate's experience (Frazier was a 1932 graduate). It is probable that Rushing did not understand the references ("Rinehart, Rinehart, I'm a most indifferent guy"), but the overall impact of the performance is undiminished. Singing over the sixteen-piece band, Rushing demonstrates the musical force heard in Bessie Smith's *St. Louis Blues* appearance. The arrangement is by saxophonist Tab Smith and features a classic two-chorus introductory solo by tenor saxophonist Don Byas. Notable as well is the obbligato part played by trombonist Dicky Wells behind Rushing's first two choruses, calling to mind the more sympathetic instrumental accompaniments on Smith's records.

Rushing was a product of the blues tradition in the Southwest, though he had enough musical knowledge and vocal flexibility to deal with a range of repertoire beyond the scope of many of his contemporaries. Although Bessie Smith never toured much beyond the Mississippi as far as we know, the influence of her recordings certainly was felt across the country. Rushing's vocal quality and shouting yet ultimately subtle delivery was definitely a product of that style. For his part, Rushing made an album in 1960 for Columbia saluting "The Smith Girls": Bessie, Clara, Mamie, and Trixie, each of whom is represented by a few signature recordings.

Big Joe Turner

Big Joe Turner has often been compared to Bessie Smith in terms of his full-throated, shouting delivery that was meant to fill a large theater or a noisy barroom. Turner (1911–1985) was born and raised in Kansas City and was an integral part of the active jazz and blues scene there in the 1930s. Working as a bartender, he would improvise blues lyrics over the boogie-woogie piano playing of Pete Johnson, with whom he had a professional partnership that lasted decades. By the late 1930s, they were both in New York where they found success together and separately, making numerous recordings of usually fast-paced blues with a heavy beat. After a short stint onstage with Duke Ellington's revue *Jump for Joy*, he settled in Los Angeles and began making blues records for small labels that began to find popularity. Turner spent much of the 1950s recording more popular-oriented rhythm and blues material such as "Chains of Love" and "Shake, Rattle, and Roll," which became important influences in the rise of rock and roll.

After making good money on a number of hit records, Turner returned to recording with smaller jazz and blues combos by the final years of the decade (a pattern he continued for the rest of his life). One especially notable record was *Big Joe Rides Again* (Atlantic LP 1332, released in 1959). This featured him fronting a first-class jazz group including Coleman Hawkins on tenor sax, Jimmy Jones on piano, Jim Hall on guitar, and Vic Dickenson on trombone playing Ernie Wilkins arrangements about equally divided between standards and blues tunes associated with Turner. One of the former was "Time after Time," a sophisticated ballad composed by Sammy Cahn and Jule Stein to be sung by Frank Sinatra in the 1947 film *It Happened in Brooklyn*.

The fact that Turner was given this to record (as well as a few other pop tunes of earlier vintage) suggests that his repertoire, like Bessie Smith's, could never be defined by blues alone. Reminiscences by several people who heard her singing in the 1930s said she was introducing new tunes at her shows all the time, including ballads such as "Stardust" and "Smoke Gets in Your Eyes." We have seen from an examination of her performances of more complex show tunes with James P. Johnson that she could handle such material without losing the stylistic devices that made her so unique. Likewise, Joe Turner could take a tune like "Time after Time" and make it his own by incorporating the signature elements of his performance style.

After a short piano introduction by Jones that is very much in the late 1950s hard bop ballad idiom, Turner enters singing the chorus over Wilkins's arrangement for four horns featuring numerous bop touches, although he makes no concession to modernity in the sense of singing anything but melody. He does, however, incorporate numerous bluesy touches: bent notes, melisma, and ornaments that were all common to Bessie Smith as well. A half chorus solo by the ageless Coleman Hawkins follows and Turner sings it out, calling to mind a gospel performance.

Turner was another of the singers under discussion who had gospel roots before turning to more vernacular styles of music, but the style remained with him, as it did with Smith. It is intriguing to think that this might have been how she would have treated some of those more sophisticated songs she was singing by the early 1930s. Her response to the more modern accompaniment in her last session has been discussed, and it is reasonable to think that, had she lived, she would have been singing songs like "Time after Time."

Bob Wills

A contemporary of both Rushing and Turner but one who operated in a very different marketplace was Bob Wills (1905–1975). A son of a white cotton planter who was also a fiddler, Wills learned violin and other string instruments as a boy. Growing up in the Texas Panhandle, he was in constant contact with African American families and culture, particularly music, for which he maintained an affinity his entire life. In interviews later in life, he never stopped praising Bessie Smith and once said he rode fifty miles to hear her sing in the 1920s (Townsend 1986, 36). He came to an understanding of black music in general and blues in particular that was well beyond most of the white musicians playing what was then called "hillbilly" music.

By the time he was in his mid-teens he was hoboing around the Southwest, performing music along with comedy and dancing and basically acting as a white minstrel by the time he settled in Fort Worth in the late 1920s. At this point he began playing in a string group called the Light Crust Doughboys, which was featured on a regular radio program from 1930 to 1933. Following this, he formed his own group, the Texas Playboys, which gradually began to incorporate more popular music influence in repertoire and instrumentation. By the late 1930s, it included Wills on violin along with another violin, piano, rhythm guitar, steel guitar, bass, drums, and a horn section of one or two trumpets and one to three reeds.

Wills expressed the idea that he wanted to cross over from the traditional country music of the string bands to a more contemporary pop sound using drums and horns. The repertoire on his recordings from the first five or six years included a high percentage of pop tunes and jazz standards, albeit mostly from the previous decade, including several songs he took from Bessie Smith recordings. One of the most intriguing was his version of "Empty Bed Blues" (Columbia 20228, May 17, 1938).

This recording features a vocal by pianist Tommy Duncan, who sings the first two choruses Smith uses on the second side of her version and then takes one from the first part ("I'm a deep-sea diver got a stroke that can't go wrong") before singing the final one. The quicker tempo allows for instrumental solos—a piano solo by Al Stricklin clearly showing the influence of Jess Stacy, a banjo solo by Sleepy Johnson that was a look back to the previous decade, and a modern-sounding clarinet obbligato by Charles Laughton on the final chorus. These jazz-oriented solos were innovations in country music but contributed to Wills's appeal to fans of the big bands and even traditional blues groups. He himself makes no vocal appearance (unusual during this period), although the violin accompaniment on Duncan's second chorus may be by him.

At any rate, the recording was issued by "Bob Wills and His Texas Playboys," then experiencing the first blush of commercial success that was to grow exponentially in the next decade. Wills was generally credited with being the most successful performer in the style of Western swing, which held a crossover appeal during the years following World War II, although by that time Wills had returned to a string-dominated group. It was not only his commercial success but his innovations in adding horns, improvised solos, and nontraditional repertoire that made Wills an acknowledged influence on a host of country musicians of subsequent generations including Merle Haggard, Willie Nelson, Asleep at the Wheel, and, strangely, Jimi Hendrix.

Wills's early inspiration from Bessie Smith and other African American singers of the 1920s clearly formed his musical identity and inspired his use of some of her repertoire. This respect was carried to an even greater extreme in 1974 by country singer Hoyt Axton, who recorded an entire album of Bessie Smith tunes accompanied by a band of seasoned jazz veterans, although the result suffers from Axton's eccentric approach to the material.

Nina Simone

Nina Simone (1933–2003) is surely one of the most uncategorizable singers in American popular music. Yet another example of an African American singer who began singing in church but then moved on, taking with her the lessons she learned, Simone was also a sophisticated musician with significant piano training. Simone moved to Philadelphia after going to school in North Carolina and began the process of gigging and teaching, adding singing to her accomplishments as well. After a successful first album (recorded in 1958), she signed with Colpix and recorded a series of jazz-oriented albums for them, many featuring her own piano playing as well as singing.

It is unclear how much input Simone had in determining her repertoire for these recording sessions, but she recorded at least four Bessie Smith tunes for Colpix (although at least two were not released until years later), suggesting her own choice. Over the course of her career Simone recorded at least seven tunes associated with Smith and several (such as "Gimme a Pigfoot" and "Need a Little Sugar in My Bowl") multiple times for different companies, although she, like Smith, put very little stock in the permanence of her own recorded legacy.

One of the first Classic Blues songs Simone recorded was "'Tain't Nobody's Biz-ness If I Do" (Colpix unissued, recorded 1960 or 1961), which she probably also associated with Billie Holiday, who recorded it for Decca in 1949. On this very informal track, Simone is featured on piano with her quartet, which plays it as a jam tune for the first two minutes of the track. As she enters, the tempo begins to pick up though she sings in a sparing, almost conversational manner that increases in intensity (vocally as well as instrumentally), ending each chorus as Smith did with the lyrics of the title stated in a defiant matter. For the last chorus, the tempo is slowed down by half as she turns it into a powerful, gospel-styled shout chorus bringing the performance to a thunderous conclusion.

Simone was often thought of as difficult—she had clear opinions on race, gender, and musical quality and was not afraid to express them at considerable volume. Her musical training and abilities made her very unwilling to suffer fools, and in that she and Bessie Smith were surely similar. Simone at one point fired a gun at an agent she felt was withholding money from her, a clear parallel with the story about Smith and Jack Gee throttling Clarence Williams in order to gain a release from her first contract. The way Simone conducted her professional life (and to a certain degree her personal one as well) was an outgrowth of the trails that Smith had blazed during her heyday in the 1920s and 1930s.

Janis Joplin

Few pop stars arrived on the national scene, shot to the top of the charts, and passed away more quickly than did Janis Joplin (1943–1970). A self-admitted misfit who grew up in Texas, Joplin was a white teenager who was attracted to the music of the blues queens of the 1920s, especially Bessie Smith. A small coterie of students in her high school were attracted to early blues, and Joplin responded to the sounds naturally. By 1963 she had decided that Texas did not hold many prospects for her and she relocated to San Francisco, where she began experimenting with drugs as well as appearing at coffeehouses, singing blues and folk material, while accompanying herself on guitar.

Several demo recording sessions yielded a variety of material, including several Bessie Smith tunes ("Careless Love," "Black Mountain Blues," and "Nobody Knows When You're Down and Out") and other traditional songs. In this early stage, her voice was piercing but without the raw quality that she brought to her later recordings. It was at this point that she began writing her own songs as well, although most were clearly inspired by blues and folk music, especially from the African American tradition.

After a short return to Texas to regain her health and footing, Joplin returned to the West Coast in 1966 to be the featured singer with Big Brother and the Holding Company, a blues-drenched rock band active in the psychedelic movement of the time. She recorded two albums with them, the second of which, *Cheap Thrills* (Columbia, KCS 9700, 1968), contained her own song "Turtle Blues," which she had composed several years before. This tune is as elemental as a blues can be; accompanied by only piano, guitar, bass, and drums, Joplin brings a searing intensity to the performance. Her lyrics could have been sung by Bessie Smith forty years earlier. For example,

I ain't the kind of woman who'd make your life a bed of ease, [x2]
Yeah, but if you, if you just wanna go out drinkin', honey, won't you invite me along please?
(Oh, I'll be so good to ya babe, yeah!)

Joplin uses a passionate approach. Though her voice is not a great instrument, she uses a variety of pitch alterations, growls, bends, and screams that rival Smith's library of blues effects. With no horns to answer her phrases, she answers herself in much the same way that Smith did in similar circumstances.

Joplin's influence was widespread—virtually all female rock and roll performers have acknowledged the debt they owe to her for blazing a trail for solo women performers in the new music. She had influence on men, as well, with singers like Robert Plant taking on many of her extreme vocal effects as well as her blues feeling. She was deeply impressed with Bessie Smith, not only on a musical level, but as a trailblaz-er herself. She saw Smith as an early version of herself—a young wom-an thrust into the limelight and given incredible responsibility as a performer, especially after she went out on her own as a soloist and bandleader in 1969. Although she only had a year left in her life, she packed it with recordings, live performances, and a phenomenal degree of self-abuse, further echoing Smith's influence. As one of her last acts in the summer of 1970, she and singer Juanita Hall (who did housework for Smith in the 1930s) put up the money to fund a headstone for Smith's grave, which had been unmarked since she was buried there in 1937.

CONCLUSION

As the last chapter demonstrated, Bessie Smith's influence extended far beyond her lifetime. She did not tour as far afield as did most major performers of her day (for example, she was not known to have appeared farther north than New York City or in Chicago, on the West Coast, or in the Midwest). Fortunately, she was among the first black performers who truly benefitted commercially by distribution of her recordings. The fact that she made so many further extended her influence. Touching many parts of the African American popular music experience, these records represented a broad appeal to listeners of countless different backgrounds and ethnicities. The number of tribute albums made of her music is virtually unprecedented—artists as varied as Dinah Washington, Carrie Smith, Juanita Hall, Hoyt Axton, and Ronnie Gilbert (of the Weavers) all did full-length albums of songs associated with Smith, although the quality of the settings as well as the performances themselves vary widely.

Each of the performers mentioned in chapter 8 (as well as thousands of others) found something personal in the music that Bessie Smith committed to record as well as in the way she conducted her personal dealings with the entertainment life. Her interpretation of lyrics about love, loss, and defiance was compelling in its passion as well as musicality and reflected a complex union of influences as diverse as minstrelsy, gospel, vaudeville, and popular song. Unifying it all was Bessie Smith's artistry—not just a natural gift, but an innate talent developed through years of small-time performances and interaction with a panoply of other performers, both in person and on record.

Bessie Smith probably regarded the decision not to renew her recording contract with regret; she had spent a lot of time in the Columbia studios during the course of the previous eight years and had developed an excellent and productive professional relationship with Frank Walker because of it. Nevertheless, she could not have been despondent over her fortune: her tours continued to be profitable and her personal appearances showed that she was still popular with her fan base. Other than the loss of income from the records (which by 1929 was fairly small), her life was probably not affected in the slightest—at least initially. When she died in 1937 she was on the threshold of what might have been a career resurgence (it was too soon for a renaissance). Both John Hammond and Lionel Hampton were talking about making recordings with her featuring the best of the new generation of jazz musicians, and it is probable, in Hampton's case, anyway, that the songs would have been more modern than any she had recorded to that point. Where she would have gone from there (Hollywood films, Broadway, featured with big bands, European tours, eventually television appearances) is a moot yet fascinating question that begs to be asked yet never answered.

In some ways a fitting finale came to the influential career of Bessie Smith in the summer of 2015 with the release of the HBO television movie about her life. *Bessie* starred Queen Latifah as the empress of the blues and won an Emmy for best television movie of the year. Critical opinion was generally favorable, although a highly romanticized "Hollywood" treatment was given to Smith's personal life. The music was highly praised, with Latifah's performance particularly successful in paying tribute to Smith without attempting to imitate her.

BIBLIOGRAPHY

ANNOTATED BIBLIOGRAPHY

Abbott, Lynn and Doug Seroff. *Ragged but Right: Black Traveling Show, "Coon Songs," & the Dark Pathway to Blues and Jazz.* Jackson: University of Mississippi Press, 2007.
One of a series of books and articles by these two authors, *Ragged but Right* details a largely unexplored corner of African American popular music history and recovers many of the details of how black groups toured in the first half of the twentieth century. It is a vital resource for understanding how music was used in minstrel, circus, and tent show bands and the evolution of style from minstrelsy and ragtime to blues and jazz.
Albertson, Chris. *Bessie—Revised and Expanded Edition.* New Haven, CT: Yale University Press, 2003.
Chris Albertson first published *Bessie* in 1972 after several years of voluminous research. He interviewed surviving contemporaries of Smith (most notably Ruby Walker and Maud Smith) as well as record producers and acquaintances. He also did exhaustive documentary work in black newspapers and trade journals and is responsible for a huge amount of what we know about both her personal and professional life. The 2003 reprint of the original book includes much new research and the benefit of three decades of historical perspective as well.
————. Notes to *Bessie Smith, The Complete Recordings* (six volumes). Columbia: C2K 47471, 1992.
In addition to the obvious benefit of having all Smith's recordings (as well as many alternate takes and the sound track to *St. Louis Blues*) in one place, this collection includes excellent notes that complement Albertson's book and many unpublished photographs. The final CD is a bonus, including a long composite interview with Ruby Walker.
Allen, Walter C. *Hendersonia: The Music of Fletcher Henderson and His Musicians.* Highland Park, NJ: Jazz Monographs No. 4, 1973.
Considering that all the research for this monumental work was done during the pre-Internet era, Allen's dedication and attention to detail borders on miraculous. Leaving no documentary stone unturned, he traces the Henderson band and its individual musicians virtually day by day during the career of the group, citing news articles, gossip columns, interviews, recordings, contracts, published sheet music, and tour information, giving us the most detailed biography of any popular music group in history.
Brooks, Edward. *The Bessie Smith Companion—A Critical and Detailed Appreciation of the Recordings.* New York: Da Capo Press, 1982.

Brooks was among the first to do a comprehensive, track-by-track examination of an artist's repertoire. As an encyclopedic resource it is extremely important, although many of his value judgments seem questionable at this point in the historiography.

Dixon, Robert M. W., Howard W. Rye, and John Godrich. *Blues and Gospel Records 1890–1942*. New York: Oxford University Press, 1997.

This discography is a refinement of Brian Rust's *Jazz on Record* (see below) and contains much more information on Country Blues, vaudeville, and even minstrel performers.

Foreman, Ronald Clifford. *Jazz and Race Records 1920–1932*. PhD dissertation, University of Illinois, 1968.

Foreman's dissertation is still the best source for nuts-and-bolts information on the industry of "race records." Still a neglected field of study, race records are an inseparable piece of the history of early jazz and blues.

Lord, Thomas. *The Jazz Discography* (online resource). www.lordisco.com.

This discography is also available on CD-ROM and is essentially a compilation of all the other jazz discographies available, with information on recent recordings added periodically. The great benefit is its search friendliness. Researchers can search for tunes, musicians, bands, record labels, or single issues of records. There is also a wealth of data about LP and CD reissues.

Rust, Brian. *Jazz on Record 1897–1943*. 2 vols. New York: Arlington House, 1978.

Brian Rust published a number of discographies, but this one is perhaps the most conclusive. A product of decades of research, *Jazz on Record* has never been surpassed for its information on recording data and band personnel.

Shapiro, Nat, and Nat Hentoff. *Hear Me Talkin' to Ya: The Story of Jazz as Told by the Men Who Made It*. New York: Dover Publications, 1955.

In some ways this book marks the beginning of the "in their own words" style of interview history in American popular music. The number of musicians and producers who were interviewed for this project is staggering, and the fact that so many of them would be gone within a decade makes this a vital resource for research into early jazz and blues styles.

OTHER SOURCES

Abbott, Lynn, and Doug Seroff. "Bessie Smith: The Early Years." *Blues & Rhythm* 70 (June 1992): 8–11.

———. *Out of Sight: The Rise of African American Popular Music, 1889–1895*. Jackson: University of Mississippi Press, 2002.

Anderson, Lisa M. *Mammies No More: The Changing Image of Black Women on Stage and Screen*. Lanham, MD: Rowman & Littlefield, 1997.

Antelyes, Peter. "Red Hot Mamas: Bessie Smith, Sophie Tucker, and the Ethnic Maternal Voice in American Popular Song." In *Embodied Voices—Representing Female Vocality in Western Culture*. Ed. Leslie C. Dunn and Nancy A. Jones. New York: Cambridge University Press, 1996.

Appel, Alfred, Jr. *Jazz Modernism: From Ellington and Armstrong to Matisse and Joyce*. New York: Alfred A. Knopf, 2002.

Avakian, George. "Bessie Smith." In *The Art of Jazz—Essays on the Nature and Development of Jazz*. Ed. Martin Williams. New York: Oxford University Press, 1959.

Barlow, William. *Looking Up at Down: The Emergence of Blues Culture*. Philadelphia, PA: Temple University Press, 1989.

Bernardi, Daniel. "Race and the Emergence of the U.S. Cinema." In *The Birth of Whiteness: Race and the Emergence of U.S. Cinema*. Ed. Daniel Bernardi. New Brunswick, NJ: Rutgers University Press, 1996.

Bogle, Donald. *Toms, Coons, Mulattoes, Mammies & Bucks: An Interpretive History of Blacks in American Films*. New York: Continuum Publishing, 1996.

Bradford, Perry. *Born with the Blues: Perry Bradford's Own Story*. New York: Oak Publications, 1965.

Bradley, Edwin M. *The First Hollywood Sound Shorts, 1926–1931*. Jefferson, NC: McFarland, 2005.

Brooks, Edward. *Influence and Assimilation in Louis Armstrong's Cornet and Trumpet Work (1923–1928)*. Lewiston, UK: Edwin Mellen Press, 2000.

———. *The Young Louis Armstrong on Records: A Critical Survey of the Early Recordings, 1923–1928*. Lanham, MD: Scarecrow Press, 2002.

Carby, Hazel V. "'It Jus Be's Dat Way Sometime': The Sexual Politics of Women's Blues." In *Unequal Sisters—A Multicutural Reader in U.S. Women's History*. Ed. Ellen Carol du-Bois and Vicki L. Ruiz. New York: Routledge, 1990.

Chilton, John. *Sidney Bechet—The Wizard of Jazz*. New York: Oxford University Press, 1987.

Collier, James Lincoln. *Making of Jazz: A Comprehensive History*. New York: Dell Publishing, 1978.

Courlander, Harold. *Negro Folk Music, U.S.A.* New York: Dover Publications, 1992.

Crafton, Donald. *The Talkies: American Cinema's Transition to Sound, 1926–1931*. Berkeley: University of California Press, 1999.

Cripps, Thomas. *Black Film as Genre*. Bloomington: Indiana University Press, 1978.

———. "The Making of *The Birth of a Race:* The Emerging Politics of Identity in Silent Movies." In *The Birth of Whiteness—Race and the Emergence of U.S. Cinema*. Ed. Daniel Bernardi. New Brunswick, NJ: Rutgers University Press, 1996.

———. *Slow Fade to Black: The Negro in American Film, 1900–1942*. New York: Oxford University Press, 1993.

———. "Stepin Fetchit and the Politics of Performance." In *Beyond the Stars: Studies in American Popular Film*, 35–48. Vol. 1: *Stock Characters in American Popular Film*. Ed. Paul Loukides and Linda K. Fuller. Bowling Green, OH: Bowling Green State University Popular Press, 1990.

Cullen, Frank. "Bessie Smith." *Vaudeville Times* 3, no. 3 (2000): 6–7.

Dahl, Linda. *Stormy Weather*. New York: Pantheon Books, 1984.

Davis, Angela Y. *Blues Legacies and Black Feminism*. New York: Pantheon Books, 1998.

Delson, Susan. *Dudley Murphy—Hollywood Wild Card*. Minneapolis: University of Minnesota Press, 2006.

Donald, James. "Jazz Modernism and Film Art: Dudley Murphy and *Ballet Mecanique*." *Modernism/modernity* 16, no. 1 (January 2009): 25–49.

Driggs, Frank. "Don Redman—Jazz Composer, Arranger." In *Jazz Panorama—From the Pages of the Jazz Review*. Ed. Martin Williams. New York: Da Capo Press, 1979.

Durgnat, Raymond, *The Crazy Mirror—Hollywood Comedy and the American Image*. New York: Horizon Press, 1969.

Evans, David. *Big Road Blues: Tradition & Creativity in the Folk Blues*. Berkeley, CA: Da Capo Press, 1982.

Fiddler, Harry. "Bessie Smith, Blues Singer, Auto Victim," *Chicago Defender*, October 2, 1937.

Floyd, Samuel A., Jr. "Music in the Harlem Renaissance—An Overview." In *Black Music in the Harlem Renaissance: A Collection of Essays*. Ed. Samuel A. Floyd Jr. Knoxville: University of Tennessee Press, 1993.

———. *The Power of Black Music: Interpreting Its History from Africa to the United States*. New York: Oxford University Press, 1995.

Friedman, Ryan Jay. *Hollywood's African American Films: The Transition to Sound*. New Brunswick, NJ: Rutgers University Press, 2011.

Gabbard, Krin. *Jammin' at the Margins: Jazz and the American Cinema*. Chicago: University of Chicago Press, 1996.

Gates, Henry Louis, Jr. *The Signifying Monkey: A Theory of African-American Literary Criticism*. New York: Oxford University Press, 1988.

Gottschild, Brenda Dixon. *Waltzing in the Dark: African American Vaudeville and Race Politics in the Swing Era*. New York: Palgrave, 2000.

Grainger, Porter, and Bob Ricketts. *How to Play and Sing the Blues*. New York: Jack Mills, 1927.

Hadlock, Richard. *Jazz Masters of the 1920's*. New York: MacMillan, 1968.

Hammond, John. "Bessie's Voice 'Full of Shoutin' & Moanin' & Prayin'" Was Powerful to the End." *Downbeat* (December 1937): 13.

Handy, W. C. *Father of the Blues: An Autobiography*. Ed. Arna Bontemps. New York: Da Capo, 1969.

———, ed. *A Treasury of the Blues*. New York: Simon and Schuster, 1949.

Harrison, Daphne Duvall. *Black Pearls*. New Brunswick, NJ: Rutgers University Press, 1988.

Higginbotham, Evelyn Brooks. "Rethinking Vernacular Culture: Black Religon and Race Records in the 1920's and 1930's." In *The House That Race Built*. Ed. Wahneema Lubiano. New York: Vintage Books, 1998.

Hilbert, Robert. *James P. Johnson: A Case of Mistaken Identity*. Metuchen, NJ: Scarecrow Press, 1986.

Hoffman, Frederick J. *The 20's*. New York: Free Press, 1962.

Howland, John. *"Ellington Uptown"—Duke Ellington, James P. Johnson and the Birth of Concert Jazz*. Ann Arbor: University of Michigan Press, 2009.

Hurston, Zora Neale. "Spirituals and Neo-Spirituals." In *Negro—An Anthology*. Ed. Nancy Cunard. New York: Frederick Ungar, 1933.

Hyatt, Marshall, and Cheryl Sanders. "Film as a Medium to Study the Twentieth-Century Afro-American Experience." *Journal of Negro Education* 53, no. 2 (spring 1984): 161–72.

James, David E. "Soul of the Cypress—The First Postmodernist Film?" *Film Quarterly* 56, no. 3 (spring 2003): 25–31.

Jones, G. William. *Black Cinema Treasures, Lost and Found*. Denton: University of North Texas Press, 1991.

Jones, Max, and John Chilton. *Louis: The Louis Armstrong Story, 1900–1971*. Boston: Little, Brown, 1971.

Jordan, Matthew F. *Le Jazz: Jazz and French Cultural Identity*. Urbana: University of Illinois Press, 2010.

Judd, Ann. "A Portrait of Russell Smith." *Jazz Journal* 20, no. 4 (1967).

Kelley, Robin D. G. *Race Rebels—Culture, Politics, and the Black Working Class*. New York: Fred Press, 1994.

Kenney, William Howland, III. "The Influence of Black Vaudeville on Early Jazz." *The Black Perspective in Music* 14, no. 3 (fall 1986).

———. *Recorded Music in American Life: The Phonograph and Popular Memory 1890–1945*. New York: Oxford University Press, 1999.

Knight, Athelia. "In Retrospect: Sherman H. Dudley: He Paved the Way for T.O.B.A." *Black Perspective in Music* 15, no. 2 (fall 1987).

Leab, Daniel J. *From Sambo to Superspade—The Black Experience in Motion Pictures*. Boston: Houghton Mifflin, 1975.

Leib, Sandra. *Mother of the Blues: A Study of Ma Rainey*. Amherst: University of Massachusetts Press, 1982.

Levine, Henry. "Gershwin, Handy and the Blues." *Clavier* 9, no. 7 (October 1970).

Levine, Lawrence. *Black Culture and Black Consciousness: Afro-American Folk Thought from Slavery to Freedom*. New York: Oxford University Press, 1977.

Lewis, Paul. "Blues on the Silver Screen—Bessie Smith in *St. Louis Blues* (1929)." *Blueprint* 11 (September 1993).

Liebman, Roy. *Vitaphone Films: A Catalogue of the Features and Shorts*. Jefferson, NC: McFarland, 2003.

Lindstrom, Bo, and Dan Vernhettes. *Travelling Blues: The Life and Times of Tommy Ladnier*. Paris: JazzEdit, 2009.

Lyttelton, Humphrey. *The Best of Jazz: Basin Street to Harlem*. New York: Penguin Books, 1980.

Magee, Jeffrey. *The Uncrowned King of Swing—Fletcher Henderson and Big Band Jazz*. New York: Oxford University Press, 2005.

Manatu, Norma. *African American Women and Sexuality in the Cinema*. Jefferson, NC: McFarland, 2003.

McGinley, Paige. *Staging the Blues: From Tent Show to Tourism*. Durham, NC: Duke University Press, 2014.

McGuire, Phillip. "Black Music Critics and the Classic Blues Singers." *Black Perspective in Music* 14, no. 2: 103–25 (spring 1986).

Meeker, David. *Jazz at the Movies*. New York: Da Capo, 1981.

Metzer, David. "Shadow Play: The Spiritual in Duke Ellington's 'Black and Tan Fantasy.'" *Black Music Research Journal* 17, no. 2 (autumn 1997): 137–58.

Miller, Karl Hagstrom. *Segregating Sound—Inventing Folk and Pop Music in the Age of Jim Crow*. Durham, NC: Duke University Press, 2010.

Morgenstern, Dan. "Jazz on Film." In *Living with Jazz*. Ed. Sheldon Meyer. New York: Pantheon Books, 2004.

Muir, Peter. *Long Lost Blues: Popular Blues in American, 1850–1920*. Urbana: University of Illinois Press, 2010.

Negra, Diane. *Off-White Hollywood: American Cultural and Ethnic Female Stardom*. New York: Routledge, 2001.

Oliver, Paul. *Screening the Blues: Aspects of the Blues Tradition*. New York: Da Capo, 1968.

Polillo, Arrigo, and Fred Bouchard, trans. "Bessie the Great." *Jazz Journal* 22, no. 4 (April 1969): 6–8.

Reed, Bill. *Hot from Harlem: Profiles in Classic African-American Entertainment*. Los Angeles: Cellar Door Books, 1998.

Reid, James M. "Bessie Smith Is Buried in Philadelphia," *Chicago Defender*, October 9, 1937.

Reid, Mark A. *Redefining Black Film*. Berkeley: University of California Press, 1993.

Rhodes, Chip. *Structures of the Jazz Age: Mass Culture, Progressive Education and Racial Disclosures in American Modernism*. London: Verso, 1998.

Robertson, David. *W. C. Handy—The Life and Times of the Man Who Made the Blues*. New York: Alfred A. Knopf, 2009.

Rocchio, Vincent F. *Reel Racism—Confronting Hollywood's Construction of Afro-American Culture*. Boulder, CO: Westview Press, 2000.

Russell, Michele. "Slave Codes and Liner Notes." In *All the Women Are White, All the Blacks Are Men—But Some of Us Are Brave*. Ed. Gloria T. Hull, Patricia Bell Scott, and Barbara Smith. New York: Feminist Press, 1982.

"'St. Louis Blues' on Screen Revive's Song's Popularity," *Chicago Defender*, September 14, 1929.

Schuller, Gunther. *Early Jazz: Its Roots and Musical Development*. New York: Oxford University Press, 1968.

Scott, Michelle R. *Blues Empress in Black Chattanooga—Bessie Smith and the Emerging South*. Urbana: University of Illinois Press, 2008.

Singer, Barry. *Black and Blue: The Life and Times of Andy Razaf*. New York: Schirmer Books, 1992.

Smith, David Lionel. "What Is Black Culture?" In *The House That Race Built*. Ed. Wahneema Lubiano. New York: Vintage Books, 1998.

Southern, Eileen. *The Music of Black Americans: A History*. New York: W.W. Norton, 1971.

Spearman, Rawn. "Vocal Concert Music in the Harlem Renaissance." In *Black Music in the Harlem Renaissance: A Collection of Essays*. Ed. Samuel A. Floyd Jr. Knoxville: University of Tennessee Press, 1993.

Spring, Katherine. "Pop Go the Warner Bros., et al.: Marketing Film Songs during the Coming of Sound." *Cinema Journal* 48, no. 1 (fall 2008): 68–89.

Stanfield, Peter. "An Excursion into the Lower Depths: Hollywood, Urban Primitivism, and St. Louis Blues, 1929–1937." *Cinema Journal* 41, no. 2 (winter 2002): 84–108.

Stearns, Marshall. *Story of Jazz*. New York: Oxford University Press, 1956.

Stearns, Marshall, and Jean Stearns. *Jazz Dance: The Story of American Vernacular Dance*. New York: Schirmer, 1968.

Stewart-Baxter, Derrick. *Ma Rainey and the Classic Blues Singers.* New York: Stein & Day, 1970.

Suisman, David. *Selling Sounds: The Commercial Revolution in American Music.* Cambridge, MA: Harvard University Press, 2009.

Taylor, Frank C., with Gerald Cook. *Alberta Hunter: A Celebration in Blues.* Santa Barbara, CA: Landmark Books, 1987.

Townley, Eric. "Blues for Ed Allen." *Jazz Journal* 27, no. 3 (March 1974).

Townsend, Charles. *San Antonio Rose: The Life and Music of Bob Wills.* Urbana: University of Illinois Press, 1986.

Turvey, Malcolm. "The Avant-Garde and the 'New Spirit': The Case of *Ballet Mecanique.*" October 102 (autumn 2002): 35–58.

Wald, Elijah. *Escaping the Delta: Robert Johnson and the Invention of the Blues.* New York: Amistad, 2004.

Waters, Ethel, with Charles Samuels. *His Eye Is on the Sparrow.* New York: Pyramid Books, 1967.

Watkins, Mel. *Stepin Fetchit—The Life & Times of Lincoln Perry.* New York: Pantheon Books, 2005.

Woll, Allen. *Black Musical Theatre: From Coontown to Dreamngirls.*New York: De Capo Press. 1989.

Worsfold, Sally Ann. "Empress of the Blues." *Storyville* 25 (October/November 1969): 30–31.

Yurchenko, Henrietta. "Mean Mama Blues: Bessie Smith and the Vaudeville Era." In *Music, Gender and Culture.* Ed. Marcia Herndon and Suzanne Ziegler. New York: F. Noetzel, 1990.

Zieff, Bob. "Allen, Ed(ward Clifton)." In *New Grove Dictionary of Jazz.* New York: St. Martin's Press, 1994.

———. "Ladnier, Tommy." In *New Grove Dictionary of Jazz.* New York: St. Martin's Press, 1994.

DISCOGRAPHY

This is a list of recordings mentioned in the text. All of these recordings are also accessible on Internet sites such as YouTube, Redhotjazz.com, and Naxos. For complete discographies of Bessie Smith and the Classic Blues singers, refer to the annotated bibliography.

RECORDINGS WITH BESSIE SMITH

The following is a chronological list of recordings by Bessie Smith mentioned in the text.

Bessie Smith with Clarence Williams (piano)
New York, February 16, 1923
80863-5: Downhearted Blues, Col A3844

Bessie Smith accompanied by Her Down Home Trio: Bessie Smith with Ernest Elliott (clarinet), Clarence Williams (piano), Buddy Christian (banjo)
New York, April 11, 1923
80949-3: Aggravatin' Papa, Col A3877
80950-2: Beale Street Mama, Col A3877

Bessie Smith with Clarence Williams (piano)
New York, April 26, 1923

80862-10: 'Tain't Nobody's Biz-ness If I Do, Col A3898
80865-10: Keeps on a Rainin', Col A3898

Bessie Smith with Fletcher Henderson (piano)
New York, April 28, 1923
80995-2: Mama's Got the Blues, Col A3900

Bessie Smith with Irving Johns (piano)
New York, September 21, 1923
81226-2: Jailhouse Blues, Col A4001

Bessie Smith with Irving Johns (piano); Jimmy Jones (piano) added on "St. Louis Gal"
New York, September 24, 1923
81231-3: St. Louis Gal, Col 13005-D
81232-2: Sam Jones Blues, Col 13005-D

Bessie Smith, Clara Smith with Fletcher Henderson (piano)
New York, October 4, 1923
81261-3: Far Away Blues, Col 13007-D
81262-2: I'm Going Back to My Used to Be, Col 13007-D

Bessie Smith with George Baquet (clarinet), Jimmy Jones (piano)
New York, October 15, 1923
81244-7: Whoa, Tillie! Take Your Time, Col 13000-D
81245-6: My Sweetie Went Away, Col 13000-D

Bessie Smith with Jimmy Jones (piano), Harry Reser (guitar)
New York, January 8, 1924
81464-4: Frosty Mornin' Blues, Col 14005-D

Bessie Smith with Don Redman (clarinet), Fletcher Henderson (piano)
New York, January 9, 1924
81466-1: Haunted House Blues, Col 14010-D
81469-2: Eavesdropper's Blues, Col 14010-D

Bessie Smith with Jimmy Jones (piano), Harry Reser (guitar)
New York, January 10, 1924

81470-4: Easy Come, Easy Go Blues, Col 14005-D

Bessie Smith with Robert Robbins (violin); John Griffin (guitar) on "Sorrowful Blues"; Irving Johns (piano) on "Pinchbacks"
New York, April 4, 1924
81664-1: Sorrowful Blues, Col 14020-D
81668-3: Pinchbacks—Take 'Em Away, Col 14025-D
New York, April 5, 1924, with Robbins and Johns
81670-2: Ticket Agent, Ease Your Window, Col 14025-D
New York, April 7, 1924, with Johns
81671-3: Bo-weavil Blues, Col 14018-D

Bessie Smith with Don Redman (alto sax), Fletcher Henderson (piano)
New York, July 22, 1924
81881-1: Lou'siana Low-down Blues, Col 14031-D

Bessie Smith with Charlie Green (trombone), Fletcher Henderson (piano)
New York, July 23, 1924
81883-2: Work House Blues, Col 14032-D

Bessie Smith with Joe Smith (cornet), Charlie Green (trombone), Fletcher Henderson (piano)
New York, September 26, 1924
140062-2: Weeping Willow Blues, Col 14042-D
140063-3: The Bye Bye Blues, Col 14042-D
B140174-4: Sing Sing Prison Blues, Col 14051-D

Bessie Smith with Louis Armstrong (cornet), Fred Longshaw (harmonium)
New York, January 14, 1925
140241-1: The St. Louis Blues, Col 14064-D
140242-1: Reckless Blues, Col 14056-D
140250-2: Cold In Hand Blues, Col 140464-D

Bessie Smith with Henderson's Hot Six: Bessie Smith with Joe Smith (cornet), Charlie Green (trombone), Coleman Hawkins (clarinet),

Fletcher Henderson (piano), Charlie Dixon (banjo), Bob Escudero
(tuba)
New York, May 5, 1925
140585-2: Cake Walkin' Babies from Home, Col 35673

Bessie Smith and Her Blue Boys: Bessie Smith with same personnel
except Buster Bailey replaces Hawkins on clarinet
New York, May 6, 1925
140586-1: The Yellow Dog Blues, Col 14075-D

Bessie Smith with Louis Armstrong (cornet), Charlie Green (trombone), Fred Longshaw (piano)
New York, May 26, 1925
140626-1: Careless Love Blues, Col 14083-D
New York, May 27, 1925
140629-2: J. C. Holmes Blues, Col 14095-D
140630-1: I Ain't Going to Play No Second Fiddle, Col 14090-D

Bessie Smith/Clara Smith Vocal Duets: Bessie Smith with Clara Smith
(vocal), Stanley Miller (piano)
New York, September 1, 1925
140890-2: My Man Blues, Col 14098-D

Bessie Smith with Buster Bailey (clarinet), Fletcher Henderson (piano)
New York, March 18, 1926
141819-2: Jazzbo Brown from Memphis Town, Col 14133-D
141820-3: The Gin House Blues, Col 14158-D

Bessie Smith with Joe Smith (cornet), Fletcher Henderson (piano)
New York, May 4, 1926
142147-2: Baby Doll, Col 14147-D

Bessie Smith and Her Blue Boys: Joe Smith (cornet), Buster Bailey
(clarinet), Fletcher Henderson (piano)
New York, October 26, 1926
142876-2: One and Two Blues, Col 14172-D

Bessie Smith with James P. Johnson (piano)

New York, February 17, 1927
143490-2: Preachin' the Blues, Col 14195-D
143491-1: Back Water Blues, Col 14195-D

Bessie Smith and Her Band: Bessie Smith with Joe Smith (cornet), Jimmy Harrison (trombone), Buster Bailey (clarinet on all but "Alexander's Ragtime Band"), Coleman Hawkins (clarinet on "Alexander's Ragtime Band and "Muddy Water"), Fletcher Henderson (piano), Charlie Dixon (banjo)
   New York, March 2, 1927
   143567-2: After You've Gone, Col 14197-D
   143568-1: Alexander's Ragtime Band, Col 14219-D
   143569-2: Muddy Water, Col 14197-D
   143570-2: There'll Be a Hot Time in the Old Town Tonight, Col 14219-D

Bessie Smith and Her Blue Boys: Bessie Smith with Joe Smith (cornet), Charlie Green (trombone), Fletcher Henderson (piano)
   New York, March 3, 1927
   143575-3: Trombone Cholly, Col 14232-D
   143576-2: Send Me to the 'Lectric Chair, Col 14209-D
   143583-2: Them's Graveyard Words, Col 14209-D
   143584-2: Hot Spring Blues, Col 14569-D

Bessie Smith with James P. Johnson (piano)
   New York, April 1, 1927
   143735-3: Sweet Mistreater, Col 14260-D
   143736-3: Lock and Key, Col 14232-D

Bessie Smith with Porter Grainger (piano) Lincoln M. Conaway (guitar)
   New York, September 27, 1927
   144796-3: Mean Old Bed Bug Blues, Col 14250-D
   144797-3: A Good Man Is Hard to Find, Col 14250-D

Bessie Smith with Tommy Ladnier (cornet), Fletcher Henderson (piano), June Cole (tuba)
   New York, October 27, 1927
   144918-1: Dyin' by the Hour, Col 14273-D

144919-3: Foolish Man Blues, Col 14273-D

Bessie Smith with Demas Dean (cornet), Charlie Green (trombone), Fred Longshaw (piano)
   New York, February 21, 1928
   145670-1: Standin' in the Rain Blues, Col 14338-D

Bessie Smith with Charlie Green (trombone), Porter Grainger (piano)
   New York, March 20, 1928
   145785-3: Empty Bed Blues (pt. 1 & 2), Col 14312-D

Bessie Smith with Joe Williams (trombone), Porter Grainger (piano)
   New York, August 25, 1928
   146896-2: Please Help Me Get Him off My Mind, Col 14375-D
   146897-3: Me and My Gin, Col 14381-D

Bessie Smith with Clarence Williams (piano), Eddie Lang (guitar)
   New York, May 8, 1929
   148485-3: I'm Wild about That Thing, Col 14427-D
   148486-2: You've Got to Give Me Some, Col 14427-D
   148487-4: Kitchen Man, Col 14435-D

Bessie Smith with Ed Allen (cornet), Garvin Bushell (alto sax), Greely Walton (tenor sax), Clarence Williams (piano), Cyrus St. Clair (tuba)
   New York, May 15, 1929
   148533-2: I Got What It Takes, Col 14435-D
   148534-3: Nobody Knows You When You're Down and Out, Col 14451-D

Bessie Smith with James P. Johnson and His Orchestra: Joe Smith, Sidney DeParis (trumpet), Charlie Green (trombone), Arville Harris (clarinet/alto sax), possibly Cecil Scott (clarinet/alto sax), Happy Caldwell (clarinet/tenor sax), James P. Johnson (piano), Bernard Addison (guitar), Harry Hull (bass), Kaiser Marshall (drums), with the Hall Johnson Choir (mixed vocal chorus)
   Film sound track, New York, late June 1929
   NY-39: St. Louis Blues (part 1)
   NY-40: St. Louis Blues (part 2)

NY-41: St. Louis Blues (part 3)
NY-42: St. Louis Blues (part 4)

Bessie Smith with James P. Johnson (piano)
New York, August 20, 1929
148902-2: He's Got Me Goin', Col 14464-D
148904-1: It Makes My Love Come Down, Col 14464-D
New York, October 1, 1929
149074-3: Wasted Life Blues, Col 14476-D
149075-1: Dirty No-gooder's Blues, Col 14476-D
New York, October 11, 1929
149134-3: Blue Spirit Blues, Col 14527-D
149135-3: Worn Out Papa Blues, Col 14527-D
149136-2: You Don't Understand, Col 14487-D
149137-2: Don't Cry Baby, Col 14487-D

Bessie Smith with Louis Bacon (trumpet), Charlie Green (trombone), Garvin Bushell (clarinet), Clarence Williams (piano)
New York, March 27, 1930
150132-2: New Orleans Hop Scop Blues, Col 14516-D

Bessie Smith with James P. Johnson (piano), the Bessemer Singers (vocal quartet)
New York, June 9, 1930
150574-4: On Revival Day (rhythmic spiritual), Col 14538-D
150575-4: Moan You Mourners, Col 14538-D

Bessie Smith with Ed Allen (cornet), Steve Stevens (piano)
New York, July 22, 1930
150657-1: Hustlin' Dan, Col 14554-D
150658-2: Black Mountain Blues, Col 14554-D

Bessie Smith with Clarence Williams (piano)
New York, November 20, 1931
151883-1: Need A Little Sugar In My Bowl, Col 14634-D

Bessie Smith accompanied by Buck and His Band: Bessie Smith with Frank Newton (trumpet), Jack Teagarden (trombone), Benny Good-

man (clarinet on "Gimme a Pigfoot"), Chu Berry (tenor sax), Buck
Washington (piano), Bobby Johnson (guitar), Billy Taylor Sr. (bass)
   New York, November 24, 1933
   152577-2: Do Your Duty, Okeh 8945
   152578-2: Gimme a Pigfoot, Okeh 8949
   152579-2: Take Me for a Buggy Ride, Okeh 8949
   152580-2: I'm Down in the Dumps, Okeh 8945

OTHER RECORDINGS

The following is an alphabetical list of recordings by other artists mentioned in the text.

Mildred Bailey and Her Alley Cats: Bunny Berigan (trumpet), Johnny
Hodges (alto sax), Teddy Wilson (piano), Grachan Moncur (bass)
   New York, December 6, 1935
   60204-A: Down-hearted Blues, Par (E)R-2257

Esther Bigeou with unknown orchestra
   New York, October 5, 1921
   70224-A: The St. Louis Blues, Okeh 8026

The Boswell Sisters (vcl.) acc. by Victor Young (cond.) orchestra
   New York, May 28, 1935
   17646-2: St. Louis Blues, Br 7467

Butterbeans and Susie: Jody "Butterbeans" Edwards, Susie Edwards
with King Oliver (cornet), and Clarence Williams (piano)
   New York, September 12, 1924
   72816-B: Kiss Me Sweet, OK 8182

Lt. Jim Europe's 369th Infantry "Hell Fighters" Band: probable personnel includes Frank De Braithe, Russell Smith, Pops Foster, Jake Porter
(cornet), Dope Andrews, Herb Flemming (trombone), Pinkhead Parker (alto sax), Noble Sissle (violin), Battle Axe Kenny, Herbert Wright
(drums), clarinets, low brass, etc.

New York, March 3, 1919
67486: Memphis Blues, Pathe 22085

These Are the Blues: Ella Fitzgerald with Roy Eldridge (trumpet), Wild
Bill Davis (organ), Herb Ellis (guitar), Ray Brown (bass), Gus Johnson
(drums)
New York, October 28, 1963
63VK677: Jailhouse Blues, Verve V-4062

Emma Gover with Fletcher Henderson (piano)
New York, June 19, 1923
70232: Downhearted Blues, Pathe-Act 021006

Handy's Orchestra: unknown personnel
New York, ca. June 4, 1923
71601-B: Memphis Blues, Okeh 4896

Lillian Harris with the New Orleans Jazz Band: Dick Landon or Ells-
worth Evans (cornet), Andy Russo (trombone), Sidney Arodin (clarinet), Allie Hammed (piano), Tom de Rose (drums)
New York, ca. late May 1923
5187-4, 5: Downhearted Blues, Ban 1224

Marion Harris with unknown orchestra
New York, April 16, 1920
79124: St. Louis Blues, Col A2944

Lucille Hegamin with J. Russell Robinson (piano)
New York, June 1923
554-A: Downhearted Blues, Cameo 381

Billie Holiday with Orchestra: Frank Newton (trumpet), Tab Smith
(alto and soprano sax), Kenneth Hollon, Stanley Payne (tenor sax), Son-
ny White (piano), Jimmy McLin (guitar), Johnny Williams (bass), Eddie
Dougherty (drums)
New York, April 20, 1939
WP24403-B: Strange Fruit, Com 526
WP24405-A: Fine and Mellow, Com 526

Alberta Hunter with orchestra
    New York, early July 1922
    1105: Downhearted Blues, Para 12005

Lulu Jackson (vocal and guitar)
    Indianapolis, Indiana, June 21, 1928
    E7477: Careless Love, Voc 1193

Mahalia Jackson
    Newport, Rhode Island, July 6, 1958
    ????: He's Got the Whole World in His Hands, Philips 429.583BE

Maggie Jones with Fletcher Henderson's Hot Six: Joe Smith (cornet), Charlie Green (trombone), Buster Bailey (clarinet), Fletcher Henderson (piano), Charlie Dixon (banjo)
    New York, May 5, 1925
    140583-1, 3: Cheatin' on Me, Col 14074-D
    140584-1: Mamma (Won't You Come and Ma-ma Me), —

Janis Joplin with Big Brother and the Holding Company *Cheap Thrills*
    David Getz (piano), James Gurley, Sam Andrew (guitar), Peter Albin (bass) 1968
    ???: Turtle Blues, Columbia, KCS 9700

Hazel Meyers with unknown piano
    New York, ca. December 1923
    ???: Downhearted Blues, Bell P255

Monette Moore with Clarence M. Jones (piano)
    New York, January 1923
    5053: Downhearted Blues, Para 12030

Ma Rainey with Lovie Austin and Her Blues Serenaders: Tommy Ladnier (cornet), Jimmy O'Bryant (clarinet), Lovie Austin (piano)
    Chicago, December 1923
    1597-2: Bo-weavil Blues, Para 12080

Ma Rainey and Her Georgia Band: Shirley Clay (cornet), Kid Ory (trombone), Claude "Hop" Hopson (piano), unknown banjo and tuba
> Chicago, ca. August 1927
> 4683-2: Blues Oh Blues, Para 12566

Ma Rainey with Shirley Clay (cornet), Albert Wynn (trombone), poss. Artie Starks (clarinet) piano, drums
> Chicago, ca. December 1927
> 20233-1: New Bo-weavil Blues, Para 12603

Jimmy Rushing with Count Basie and His Orchestra: Buck Clayton, Harry "Sweets" Edison, Al Killian, Ed Lewis (trumpet), Dicky Wells, Robert Scott, Eli Robinson (trombone), Earl Warren, Tab Smith (alto sax), Buddy Tate, Don Byas (tenor sax), Jack Washington (baritone sax), Count Basie (piano), Freddie Green (guitar), Walter Page (bass), Jo Jones (drums)
> New York, November 17, 1941
> 31768-1: Harvard Blues, OKeh 6564

Nina Simone (vocal and piano) with Al Shackman (guitar), Chris White (bass), Bobby Hamilton (drums)
> New York, 1960–1961
> ??: 'Tain't Nobody's Biz-ness If I Do, Blue Note 4-73217-2

Joseph C. Smith's Orchestra: Bill Hall (trumpet), Harry Raderman (tb), Max Flaster (alto sax), Joseph C. Smith (violin), Harry Akst, Hugo Frey (piano) drums
> New York, October 1, 1919
> 23282-1: Yellow Dog Blues (intro "Hooking Cow Blues"), Vic 18618

Mamie Smith accompanied by Hagar's
> New York, February 14, 1920
> 7275-E: That Thing Called Love, Okeh 4113
> 7276-D: You Can't Keep a Good Man Down

Mamie Smith and Her Jazz Hounds: Mamie Smith with Johnny Dunn (cornet), Dope Andrews (trombone), Ernest Elliott (clarinet), Willie "the Lion" Smith (piano), Leroy Parker (violin), probably others
> New York, August 10, 1920

7529-C: Crazy Blues, Okeh 4169

Ruby Smith (Ruby Walker) with Jimmy Johnson and His Orchestra: Henry "Red" Allen (trumpet), J. C. Higginbotham (trombone), Gene Sedric (tenor sax), James P. Johnson (piano), Al Casey (guitar), Johnny Williams (bass), Sidney Catlett (drums)
　　New York, March 9, 1939
　　W24207-1: Back Water Blues, Voc 4903

Trixie Smith with unknown orchestra, possibly including James P. Johnson (piano)
　　New York, ca. late January 1922
　　P-162-1: Trixie's Blues, Black Swan 2039

Mary Straine with Fletcher Henderson (piano)
　　Long Island City, ca. April 1923
　　????: Downhearted Blues, Black Swan 14150

Eva Taylor with Clarence Williams (piano)
　　New York, ca. January 10, 1923
　　71162-C: Downhearted Blues, Okeh 8047

Sophie Tucker with Miff Mole's Molers: Red Nichols (cornet), Miff Mole (trombone), Jimmy Dorsey (clarinet/alto sax), Ted Shapiro (piano), Eddie Lang (guitar), Joe Tarto (tuba), Vic Berton (drums)
　　New York, April 11, 1927
　　80716-B: After You've Gone, Okeh 40837

Big Joe Rides Again: Big Joe Turner with Ernie Royal (trumpet), Vic Dickenson (trombone), Jerome Richardson (alto sax), Coleman Hawkins (tenor sax), Jimmy Jones (piano), Jim Hall (guitar), Doug Watkins (bass), Charlie Persip (drums), Ernie Wilkins (arranger)
　　New York, September 10, 1959
　　3742: Time after Time, Atl LP(SD)1332

Victor Military Band
　　New York, July 15, 1914
　　15065-3: The Memphis Blues, Vic 17619

Dinah Washington with Fortunatus "Fip" Ricard (trumpet), Julian Priester (trombone), Eddie Chamblee (tenor sax), Charles Davis (baritone sax), Jack Wilson (piano), Robert Lee Wilson (bass), James Slaughter (drums), Robare Edmonson (arranger)
Chicago, January 7, 1958
16729: Me and My Gin, EmArcy MG36130

Ethel Waters with Her Plantation Orchestra: Harry Tate, Horace Holmes (cornet), Joe King (trombone) 2 reeds, Lester Armstead (piano), Maceo Jefferson (banjo), Bill Benford (tuba), Jesse Baltimore (drums), Ralph "Shrimp" Jones (violin)
New York, October 20, 1925
141164-2: Dinah, Col 487

Clarence Williams' Trio: Louis Armstrong (cornet), Clarence Williams (piano/vocal), Buddy Christian (banjo), Eva Taylor, Clarence Todd (vocal)
New York, October 16, 1925
73721-A: Santa Claus Blues, Okeh 8254

Bob Wills and His Texas Playboys: Tommy Duncan (vocal) with Everett Stover (trumpet), Charles Laughton (clarinet), Zeb McNally (tenor sax), Al Stricklin (piano), Eldon Shamblin (guitar), Leon McAuliffe (steel guitar), Sleepy Johnson (banjo), Joe Ferguson (bass), Jesse Ashlock, Bob Wills (violin), Smokey Dacus (drums)
DAL 583: Empty Bed Blues, CQ9070

INDEX

ABOUT THE AUTHOR

John Clark is a musicologist and performing musician in the Boston area. He has been doing freelance college teaching since 2005, primarily as a visiting assistant professor at Connecticut College. He is also a busy saxophone teacher and performer and has lead his own Wolverine Jazz Band since 1995, playing numerous national jazz festivals and concerts. He received his PhD from Brandeis University in 2004 in musicology, concentrating in American music, and has been published in *American Music, The International Association of Jazz Record Collectors Journal, The Journal of the Music Library Association*, and elsewhere.